Irish

Heroes & Heroines

of America

150 True Stories of Irish American Heroism

Frederick Fell Publishers, Inc.
2131 Hollywood Blvd., Suite 305, Hollywood, FL 33020
Phone: (954) 925-5242   Fax: (954) 925-5244
Web Site: www.FellPub.com

Frederick Fell Publishers, Inc.

2131 Hollywood Boulevard, Suite 305

Hollywood, Florida 33020

954-925-5242

e-mail: fellpub@aol.com

Visit our Web site at www.fellpub.com

Library of Congress Cataloging-in-Publication Data

Bartimole, John E., 1954-
  Irish heroes and heroines of America : 150 true stories of Irish American heroism.
      p. cm.
   ISBN 0-88391-010-1 (trade pbk. : alk. paper)
   1. Irish Americans--Biography. 2. Heroes--United States--Biography. 3. Women heroes--United States--Biography. 4. Courage--United States--Anecdotes. I. Title.
   E184.I6B275 2004
   973'.049162--dc22

                                    2004007142

10 9 8 7 6 5 4 3 2 1
Graphic Design: Chris Hetzer

Table of Contents

Introduction

Irish Heroes & Heroines of America

Introduction & Acknowledgments

No introduction can do justice to the role of the people of Iris descent have played in history, and I won't try to do that in this space. I prefer to let their stories—told on the pages that follow—awash you in the richness and depth of the contributions of Irish people to the world.

Instead, I will take this opportunity to thank three remarkable individuals whose enormous talents have contributed mightily to this book: Darrell Klute, whose research and writing skills are extraordinary and are reflected throughout a majority of this book; Carole McNall, whose talents and advice are deeply appreciated; and Tracy Riordan, who came along to save me during a very difficult deadline time.

Enjoy this book. It is a story of a culture, of a people, of a history. It is a celebration of the Irish in the world, and it is a celebration of life itself.

1

Sixty-Ninth New York State Volunteer Regiment, Company A

Famed Military Unit

F rom the roots of a New York City militia squad known as the Second Regiment of Irish Volunteers, the 69th New York State Volunteer Regiment was born. The group served the United States in the American Revolution and the War of 1812. On October 12, 1851, the group was officially designated the 69th Regiment.

As Fort Sumter was bombed, President Abraham Lincoln called on the group (at the time called the New York State Militia) to fight at the First Battle of Bull Run under General William Sherman. The unit fought with distinction as the rear guard of the Federal withdrawal.

It returned home after 90 days, and two branches were formed - one being the 69th New York State Volunteers. It combined with two other predominantly Irish units to create the "Irish Brigade."

General Thomas Francis Meagher, who had been exiled to Tazmania for his anti-British activities, took charge of the 69th

NYSV. Under his leadership, the regiment was widely known for its hard fighting and luxurious camps. The Irish Brigade was remembered by General Robert E. Lee as, "That Fighting 69th."

The Battle of Antietam on September 17, 1862, and the Battle of Gettysburg from July 1-3, 1863, might be what the regiment is most remembered for. By the end of the Civil War, when they were fighting under the command of General Ulysses S. Grant, the Irish Brigade fought with distinction in nearly every major theater. The Union Army was comprised of 2,000 regiments. The 69th ranked sixth in losses and was arguably the best from New York State.

The roots of Ireland and its immigrants to America played a major role in preserving and planting more seeds for the United States.

2

Lucille D. Ball

Entertainer

Through an impressive blend of grit and wackiness, Lucille Ball propelled herself from the bluecollar grind of smalltown Western New York into the hearts of fans across the United States.

Born on August 6, 1911, of mixed Irish, Scottish, English and French descent, Lucille Désirée Ball amused herself from a very early age with the vaudeville shows and movies shown in nearby Jamestown, N.Y. Her grandmother would take her to the shows and then become her partner for sketches the young girl would base on the performances.

A born entertainer, Ball would work doggedly on high school productions; once reportedly playing the lead in, directing, casting, selling the tickets and creating posters for a performance of Charley's Aunt.

Like most aspiring actresses, she made for New York City. She proceeded to fall flat on her face at the John Murray Anderson-Robert Milton Dramatic School, feeling "terrified and useless" in the shadow of the school's brilliant pupil, Bette Davis.

After a dehabilitating bout with rheumatoid arthritis, Ball finally got national exposure -- as the Chesterfield Cigarette Girl. While the experience was not what she had in mind when coming to the Big Apple, the ad paid off. She was a last minute replacement for a minor role in the film Roman Scandals [1933].

Ball's first 18 months in Hollywood led to a series of brief appearances and minor roles in a number of films under contract with Goldwyn-United Artists. She jumped ship to the Columbia studios, sensing comedy might be her forté. She appeared in short comedies with the Three Stooges and had

3

tiny parts in feature-length films. She finally won her first screen cred-it in the 1935 release Carnival. The next seven years won her the dubi-ous honor "Queen of the Bs."

Decided to no longer be "a showgirl in a background," in the 1936 release The Girl From Paris, she stepped up to second lead, setting the stage for her leading role in the Broadway-bound musical Hey Diddle Diddle. Despite her growing success, hardship struck once again when the show closed with the death of its star, Conway Tearle.

Nearly all of her 22 releases over the next six years were unremark-able, save the musical Too Many Girls; it was on the set of this Rodgers-Hart adaptation that the young woman met the man who would be her husband and partner, Desi Arnaz. They were married on Nov. 30, 1940.

By 1943, she had shed her B-movie rap and starred opposite Red Skelton in the Cole Porter musical DuBarry Was a Lady.

Becoming disgruntled with the cinema, which she called mostly "mediocre," she accepted a radio role the CBS radio show My Favorite Husband in 1947. As a precursor to her mass popularity, she played a featherbrained wife of a midwestern banker.

Ball and Arnaz subsequently went on a nationwide vaudeville tour which would lay the foundation for I Love Lucy, which debuted on Oct. 15, 1951. The CBS show was immediately noteworthy for its production innovations. Each episode was filmed in sequence in front of a live audience, like a theatre presentation. The show's three-cam-era filming technique was also revolutionary.

Ball had finally reached the pinnacle of success: I Love Lucy was rated the number one show on television within six months. Along the way it won more than 200 awards, including five Emmys among its 23 nominations. It was named one of TV's four "all-time hits." The show was such a phenomenon that the episode featuring the birth of Little Ricky drew more viewers than the inauguration of president Dwight D. Eisenhower.

3

John Barry

Naval Captain, Revolutionary War Hero

J ohn Barry loved the sea and made it his career very early in his youth, leaving his home of Tacumshane, Ireland, at a very early age and settling in 1760 near Philadelphia when he was only 15. He quickly became wealthy as a shipmaster and as an owner.

When the winds of the Revolutionary War swirled, he enthusiastically embraced the cause of the colonists, quickly offering his services to the Continental Congress. He was placed in command of the Lexington, and scored the first capture of a British warship by a commissioned colony cruiser.

In reward, he was given command of the larger, 32-gun Effingham, which was long relegated to its harbor because of the occupation of Philadelphia by the British in 1777 and by the British Army's strong presence in Delaware; undaunted, Barry took four small boats and seized a large quantity of supplies intended for a British Army. So important was the deed that General George Washington personally congratulated Barry for his "gallantry and address."

When he finally freed the Effingham from Philadelphia, he and his crew were an important factor in the Trenton campaign; however, in

1778, he was forced to burn the ship to prevent her from being seized by the British.

Still, he persevered, commanding the 32-Raleigh and then the Alliance, also 32 guns; with the Alliance, he captured the British vessels Atlanta and Trepassy, though he was seriously wounded in the battle.

After the Revolutionary War, he was called on again to help the fledgling country, this time to fight the menace of Algerine pirates. Barry, then regarded as "...the one (naval captain) who possessed the greatest reputation for experience, conduct and skill..." was placed in command of the 44-gun United States and was crucial in defusing that threat.

He went to the West Indies in 1798 and was placed in charge of all the naval forces in that area in May of 1799. He later took command of the Guadeloupe station in the West Indies, where he remained until 1801. Two years later, he died. Though he was married twice, he left no children.

He is considered by historians to be the Revolutionary naval captain whose reputation is second only to the legendary John Paul Jones; indeed, Barry is a man whose courage, skill and cunning played a major role in the birth of the United States.

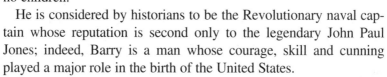

4

Mathew B. Brady

Photography Pioneer

The first thing unusual about Mathew B. Brady was his self-styled spelling of his first name--he insisted on just one "t". Even more unusual his claim that he didn't know what his middle initial stood for.

Beyond those slight eccentricities, what is known about Brady is that he was a genius, a pioneer and a very courageous man--a man whose daring and vision not only helped invent the art of photography, but which also left this country with its first photographic history of a war.

Mathew Brady is perhaps best known for his historic work, "Brady's National Photographic Collection of War Views and Portraits of Representative Men," published in 1870 as a pictorial essay of the Civil War. That project became possible when he convinced President Abraham Lincoln and Alan Pinkerton, the person in charge of the Secret Service, to allow him and his assistants to photograph battle and camp scenes of the war--very often at the risk of their own lives. Reportedly, Brady took more than 3,500 photographs, 2,000 of which were purchased by the U.S. Government for $25,000 in 1875.

But Brady's contributions to the country and to photography go deeper than that accomplishment, though that is the stuff of legends. Born in Warren County, N.Y., in 1823, of an Irish father, Brady valued and gained an impressive education--if not in school, in the world outside of school.

A turning point in his life occurred when his friend, William Page, a portrait painter, introduced him to S.F. Morse, who exposed him to the just-emerging technology of photography. Brady took to the new form quickly, making several advancements and improvements himself, finally opening up his own portrait studio in New York City in 1843.

Brady's reputation for photography grew quickly, and he was soon honored by the American Institute with the receipt of the first gold medal every awarded to daguerreotypes. Thereafter, he perfected the process of making tinted daguerreotypes on ivory, and his reputation--and success--grew.

His work, "Gallery of Illustrious Americans," published in 1850, was wildly successful, and he followed up that with a collection of 48 daguerreotypes which he displayed at the 1853 World's Fair in New York City.

He converted to the wet-plate photographic method instead of the daguerreotype process in 1855 and became the country's most famous photographer--illustrating eminent Americans from all walks of life--and, in the process, became famous himself.

He has every right to be called the Father of American Photography; certainly, he developed the form of photographic journalism, and his place in American--and photographic--history is enshrined.

5

William Jennings Bryan

Political Leader

We generally do not remember the failed presidential candidates, especially long after the elections in which they ran. But William Jennings Bryan was no ordinary presidential candidate. His rare eloquence is remembered by many who could not name the man who won that race. (It was William McKinley.)

Ironically, Bryan's eloquence is best remembered in two losing causes. In 1925, he joined the prosecution of a Tennessee teacher who had violated a statute forbidding the teaching of evolution. Bryan appeared as a witness; the cross-examination by defense attorney Clarence Darrow damaged Bryan's reputation and that of his cause.

During his 1896 presidential campaign, Bryan aligned himself with those who advocated free coinage of silver. He electrified the Democratic national convention with his speech, including the vow "you shall not crucify mankind upon a cross of gold." His reward? The nomination for president, although he was just 36.

Bryan took his campaign and his ideas throughout the country, speaking with great skill. For voters, he described the voters as a struggle between rich and poor. Although he lost to McKinley, 271 electoral votes to 176, he did not lose his place on the American stage.

Little in Bryan's early background suggested his later career. He practiced law briefly in Illinois and Nebraska before entering Congress. Four years later, a failed run for the Senate sent him home to Omaha, where he became a newspaper editor.

From his college days, however, Bryan had been noted for his skill in speaking. He was not considered an original thinker, but was able to put his ideas in clear language. By 1896, that skill had made him a popular lecture at the Chautauquas.

Bryan's first defeat did not end his presidential ambitions. In 1900, the major campaign issue was American expansion, particularly the move to make the Philippines an American territory. Bryan could not convince voters to back him, and his electoral vote total sagged to 155. Again after that defeat, he continued to speak on issues through lectures and a newspaper, the Commoner, which he started in 1901.

An anti-Bryan movement kept him from the 1904 nomination, but he did influence the party platform. He campaigned for the nominee, Judge Alton B. Parker, but without enthusiasm. That feeling was shared by voters, who rejected Parker.

By 1908, Bryan's supporters had regained control of the Democratic party. They could not, however, overcome the influence of Theodore Roosevelt, who had given his blessing to William Howard Taft. Taft won, and Bryan realized he would never become president.

But his influence on the party remained. Woodrow Wilson's nomination in 1912 came through Bryan's support. Bryan became secretary of state in Wilson's cabinet, and won over State Department skeptics with his genuine willingness to work and learn. He remained a strong Wilson supporter, and could influence Congressional support for the president's measures.

But Bryan, a pacifist, left the Wilson cabinet in 1914, when the sinking of the Lusitania edged the United States toward war. He continued to support Wilson, however, and spoke for the president during the 1916 campaign.

Bryan took his eloquence to the stages of the Chautauquas throughout his career. His wife pointed out those speeches did more than keep him in the public eye -- they gave him a chance to "(listen) to the mind of America," providing him with insight into public moods that many other political leaders lacked.

6

James Buchanan

U.S. President

History remembers James Buchanan primarily for the end of his term, when he was faced with the actions that led to the start of the Civil War.

But the Buchanan administration offered more than feeble gestures before a coming crisis. Like many modern presidents, he was most interested in foreign policy. That interest sparked the attention needed to handle several foreign policy matters artfully. Among those were a treaty with China and the establishment of relations with Japan and Siam (modern Thailand). He also directed discussions to restrain the British from searching vessels in American waters and eased tensions between Britain, Nicaragua and Honduras.

However, Buchanan could not attain the one foreign policy achievement he most desired. Through his administration and earlier, as secretary of state to James K. Polk, he sought to add Cuba to the territory of the United States. His efforts toward that goal were never successful.

At home, Buchanan declined to take a position on the question of finance or the tariff. His secretary of the treasury stepped forward to assume leadership on the tariff. The resulting bill wounded the administration in the eyes of the public.

During his campaign, Buchanan had declared he would not seek re-election. He was not prepared, however, for the reaction of the

11

South to the election of his successor, Abraham Lincoln. Even before the election, military men warned the president that steps were needed to prepare for a possible secession. He initially ignored that advice, setting in motion a chain of events that led to several cabinet resignations and what was seen as a poor response to South Carolina's decision to secede.

Although he sympathized with the South, Buchanan supported the administration throughout the war. He spent much of his time defending the policies of his administration.

Buchanan, an attorney, was originally courted as a political candidate because of his debating skills. One observer notes he was attracted to the field because he deeply valued friendships and politics helped make those possible.

His first political office was a seat in the Pennsylvania House of Representatives. Although he intended to retire after a second term, he decided to remain in politics to help deal with the loss of a fiancé.

By 1820, Buchanan was a Congressman. Ten years later, he was again flirting with retirement from public service. An offer to serve as minister to Russia changed his mind, and he spent years in that country. When he returned to the United States, he became a senator from Pennsylvania, serving as a leader and spokesman for the Democratic party.

Buchanan surfaced as a presidential candidate in 1844, but lost that nomination to Polk. Again, he was not allowed to retire from public service. In gratitude for Buchanan's assistance in winning Pennsylvania votes, Polk selected Buchanan as secretary of state. The two skillfully directed foreign policy, including a strong restatement of the Monroe Doctrine, which discouraged European interference in the Americas.

Buchanan did not leave foreign policy matters when he left the Polk administration. Under President Franklin Pierce, he was named a negotiator to work on a treaty with Great Britain. When he returned to the United States in 1856, he was even more strongly considered a presidential candidate. This time, he won the nomination and the election. That earned him the dubious honor of being the president who watched regional tensions blossom into

Civil War.

7

William F. Buckley, Jr.

author, political activist

illiam F. Buckley, Jr. surely ranks as one of the most controversial, visionary and influential characters in the history of the American conservative movement. Many
observers give Buckley credit for carrying the banner for
the fledgling political party following World War II.

Born Nov. 24, 1925, the sixth of ten children in a wealthy family, Buckley learned to distinguish himself from the crowd at an early
age. He was born in New York City but moved frequently as a child,
spending a good deal of time in Britain and France.

Much of his father's haughtiness and independence rubbed off on
young William. When the lad turned eight, he sent a letter to the King
of England demanding that the country repay its war debt. Buckley's
father -- who controlled a $10 million oil empire -- encouraged such
toughness, going to such lengths as importing broncos to the family
estate to help the young ones develop ruggedness.

Buckley was to get his education at Yale after short stints at the
University of Mexico and the U.S. Army. Upon earning the rank second lieutenant, Buckley took to Yale to study history, economics and
political science. Before long, he was a notorious debater, a chairman
of the Yale Daily News and member of Skull and Bones.

After completing his B.A. in 1950, the young man stayed at Yale
to teach Spanish before becoming a covert agent in Mexico City for
the Central Intelligence Agency.

13

Now Buckley was on a roll. In 1959, Buckley rallied conservatives to bring down liberalism in his book Up From Liberalism. He began to paint the fragmented party a more handsome portrait, erasing their image as "fascists and anti-semites."

Buckley brought respectability to the movement, forming the New York Conservative party in 1961. After a poor attempt at running for mayor in 1965, Buckley turned his energies to the media. He wrote freelance for many national magazines and was carried by hundreds of newspapers as a syndicated columnist.

His show Firing Line also found great success in the early 1970s. He used his pompous self-assurance and keen wit to conduct fascinating interviews. His guests have included personalities from all walks: Billy Graham, Hugh Hefner, Groucho Marx, Muhammad Ali and Henry Kissinger. The show won an Emmy award in 1969.

By this time Buckley had written a handful of books. He returned to the U.S. to launch the magazine National Review to "revitalize the conservative position." The magazine's bold positions on controversial topics drew plenty of praise along with its detractors.

Buckley focused primarily on writing novels and providing a boost for conservative politicians over the course of the following decades, writing dozens of books and throwing his weight behind Barry Goldwater, Richard Nixon and Ronald Reagan.

8

Art Carney

Legendary Comedian

A rt Carney is one of the few individuals who can make people laugh without saying a word. Emblazoned in television history forever as the lovable sewer worker Ed Norton, Carney played the perfect, gullible foil to Jackie Gleason's Ralph Cramden in the legendary TV series, The Honeymooners.

With his deadpan stares, his rolling eyes, his easy looks of innocence--together with his incredible ability to irk Ralph Cramden--Carney left generations of viewers laughing at his antics.

Somehow, the irrepressible Norton always found a way to beguile his best friend Cramden, but he also always found a way to get back on his good side. In episode after episode, Norton would be ordered "outta here:" by the mercurial Cramden, who would later and inevitably put an arm around him and apologize.

As faithful a friend as ever depicted on TV, Norton, through the acting genius of Carney, has gone down as one of the most memorable characters ever portrayed on the screen--perhaps TV comedy's most famous and successful "second banana" ever.

His acting in The Honeymooners led to his receiving a host of Emmy Awards for his supporting actor role. But there's more to Art

Carney than his portrayal of Ed Norton, because his acting brilliance went far beyond comedy. His 1974 film, "Harry and Tonto," won him a Golden Globe Award and an Oscar for best performance by an actor. He later reunited with Gleason in 1985 for a TV movie, "Izzy and Moe," about two legendary Prohibition agents.

Carney served his country valiantly in World War II, suffering a serious leg injury shortly after he landed on the beaches of Normandy. As a result of that injury, Carney was left with a right leg that was about an inch shorter than the left.

He began perfecting his acting craft at an early age, entertaining in his family's living room in a show he creatively entitled, "Art for Art's Sake." The youngest of six boys, he embarked on his professional career by touring with Horace Heidt's band, and later played the straight man to Fred Allen, Bert Lahr and Edgar Bergen.

But it was his role as Norton that solidified his success and his enduring legacy. While his character preferred the more formal title of "underground sanitation expert," Carney himself knew well his place on the show: to make Cramden--and Gleason--look good. And he did so with aplomb and with skill, teaming up with The Great One to make one of the greatest comedy duos in the history of American television.

Today, decades after its short run on TV ended, The Honeymooners remains a classic--as does Ed Norton and the man who created him, Art Carney.

9

Daniel Carroll

Commissioner of the District of Columbia

At one time, there was no spot on the map labeled "District of Columbia." Daniel Carroll of Maryland was one of those who helped draw that spot and label its boundaries.

Carroll entered public life in 1781, when he was elected as a delegate to the Continental Congress. That Congress wrote the Articles of Confederation, and Carroll was one of the signers of that document.

Six years later, he joined many of the same people in an effort to rewrite the Articles at the Constitutional Convention. He favored a strongly centralized government and opposed having the states pay members of Congress.

Carroll's efforts to bring change to the young nation continued as the states considered ratification of the new constitution. Among his efforts was a letter to the Maryland Journal arguing against a delay in ratification.

Once the new constitution was in place, Carroll was chosen as one of Maryland's first senators. He voted for the bill to locate a capital district on the Potomac.

That support, his friendship with George Washington and his residence near the area being considered were believed factors in Washington's decision to appoint Carroll as one of three commissioners to survey and limit a part of the district territory.

Carroll remained in that position until May of 1795, when age and ill health forced him to resign.

As with many of the Maryland Carrolls, Carroll had enjoyed prosperity. But he, like others in his family, also felt the need to give back to that country. The history of Maryland and the District marks that contribution.

10

Charles Carroll

American Statesman, Signer of the Declaration of Independence

Perhaps no signer of the Declaration of Independence risked more personally than did Charles Carroll. When he signed the Declaration representing Maryland in early August of 1776, Carroll was estimated to be worth almost $2 million- a princely sum, particularly in colonial days. He willingly risked hi s entire fortune with the single stroke of a pen, and he did so with a history of passion and pride in his stance.

Not only did Carroll risk much as a signer of the Declaration, he was also the prime mover in convincing the Maryland delegation to support the United States' fledgling independence movement. As recently as January 11, 1776, the Maryland Convention specifically demanded that its delegates to the Continental Congress "to disavow, in the most solemn manner, all design in the colonies for independ- ence."

A little more than five months later, the Convention reversed itself, authorizing its delegates to "vote in declaring the United States free and independent states." Carroll, a strong proponent of the colonies' freedom, was recognized for his important role in the decision's reversal by being named a delegate to the Continental Congress.

Charles Carroll was born in 1737 and was descended from a

wealthy and politically well-connected family. His grandfather, also named Charles Carroll, sought relief from the persecution of Catholics in England by relocating to the colonies-specifically, Maryland--in 1688. A close ally of the third Lord Baltimore the elder Carroll was named attorney general by that Lord Baltimore, an important political position. Carroll of Carrollton's father, Charles Carroll of Annapolis, was also a wealthy landowner who bitterly opposed the political handicaps imposed on Catholics during that time.

At 10 years of age, Charles Carroll of Carrollton went to a school run by the Jesuit Order at Bohemia on Harmon's Manor in Maryland. Later, he went to another Jesuit school, St. Omer in French Flanders, followed by study at the college of the Jesuits at Reims. His formal education continued at the College Louis le Grand in Paris and at Bourges, where he studied civil law. When he returned to American in 1765, he was given the estate of Carrollton in Frederick County, Maryland, and became a staunch proponent of the rights of the colonists-and, ultimately, the right of the colonies to be free.

Following his role in the Declaration of Independence, Carroll was a key architect of the state of Maryland's constitution, and later served in that state's senate for a number of years, including two stints as its president. He also served his country as a member of Congress, but held a special place in his heart for his home state, resigning his U.S. Senate seat to hold his place in the Maryland senate, after the Congress passed a low disallowing concurrent service in a state legislature and Congress.

Ironically, the man who risked the most wealth by signing the Declaration of Independence holds the distinction of being the last signer to die when he passed away on November 14, 1832, leaving behind a legacy of independent pride and passion.

11

Mary Higgins Clark

Author

Mary Higgins Clark was born to Irish parents, Luke and Nora (maiden name Durkin) Higgins in New York City on December 24, 1929. Clark attended Villa Maria Academy and Ward Secretarial School before working as an advertising assistant in 1946.

Clark worked for Pan American Airlines from 1949 to 1950. While working for Pan American she met and married airline executive, Warren F. Clark in 1949. During their fifteen year marriage Clark had five children, Marilyn, Warren, David, Carol and Patricia. In 1964 her husband died leaving her to support the children on her own.

Clark, having always been interested in writing, began writing scripts for four-minute radio spots and short pieces for women's magazines to support her family. Though her first full length work, Aspire to the Heavens a biography on George Washington was not a commercial success, it showed she was capable of writing more than short stories and scripts.

Commercial success came calling with her first novel in 1975. Where are the Children? landed Clark on the best-seller list and earned her over one hundred thousand dollars in paperback royalties. Her second novel, another thriller entitled A Stranger is Watching, solidified her presence on the best seller lists, earning over a million dollars in paperback rights and became a movie in 1982 by Metro-Goldwyn-Mayer. Clark told People magazine, "The money changed my life in the nicest way, it took all the choking sensation out of paying for the kids' schools."

In 1989 Clark signed a contract with Simon & Schuster that changed the publishing world. Her $11.4 million deal was the largest ever between a writer and publisher. Clark published mysteries and suspense novels for Simon & Schuster including; The Cradle Will Fall, A Cry in the Night, Stillwatch, Weep No More, My Lady and While my Pretty One Sleeps.

Critics say the winning formula Clark uses is extraordinary events in everyday situations that the reader can relate to. Clark told the Washington Post, "I write for the mainstream. I write about nice people not looking for trouble. They find evil in their own car, home, everyday life."

Clark won the New Jersey Author Award in 1969, 1977 and 1978 for Aspire to the Heavens, Where Are the Children, and A Stranger is Watching respectively. In 1980 she was honored in France with the Grand Prix de Litterature Policiere and in 1983 she received an honorary doctorate from Villanova University.

Throughout her career Clark has served in various writers' organizations. In 1987 she served as president of the Mystery Writers of America. She belongs to Authors Guild, Authors League of America, American Academy of Arts and Sciences, American Society of Journalists and Authors and is on the executive council of the American Irish Historical Society.

12

Grover Cleveland

President- Statesman

G rover Cleveland's political supporters said they loved him "for the enemies he has made," particularly the corrupt and the dishonest.

But the voting public also loved him for the work he did. Although he lacked the electoral college votes required for a second term in 1888, popular support convinced him to try again and he returned to office in 1892. That made him the first (and, to date, only) president returned to office after four years of retirement.

Cleveland entered his first presidential campaign as his party's hope to lure Republican voters disenchanted with their nominee, James G. Blaine. The move succeeded, even though Blaine supporters threw campaign mud, including a charge that Cleveland had fathered an illegitimate child. He was elected in 1884 as the first Democratic president after the Civil War.

The new president had established a reputation as a reformer long before moving into the White House. In 1881, the Democrats nominated him as a reform candidate for mayor of Buffalo, N.Y. His efforts brought him statewide notice. Running for governor in 1882 as an "unowned candidate," he drew many Republican voters and won.

During his service as governor, Cleveland maintained his reputation for stubborn honesty, but dismayed some supporters by exercising independent judgment and refusing to play the spoils game. He joined with

23

another stubborn politician, New York City Mayor Theodore Roosevelt, to push reform efforts in the city.

As president, Cleveland continued his reform efforts by steadily pushing the work of the Civil Service Commission. Attempts to reduce tariffs and to restrict distribution of Civil War pensions to those who had truly earned them were politically dangerous but, to the president, necessary.

During his first term, Cleveland also got an early taste of the spotlight that would haunt 20th century presidents. Coverage of his marriage in 1886 to Frances Folsom left Cleveland, in the words of a biographer, outraged by the "colossal impertinence" of the press.

National finances presented the problem in Cleveland's second term. Efforts to control inflation alienated him from some in his party, and he was not nominated to run again in 1896. He retired to Princeton, N.J., but the public and fellow politicians were not ready to allow him to fade from sight.

For Cleveland, unlike some former presidents, retirement provided opportunities for service and enjoyment of life. He almost immediately received requests for speeches and articles. Princeton University made him a trustee, and President Theodore Roosevelt wanted to place him on a commission to investigate the anthracite coal strike. He also agreed to assist in the reorganization and management of the Equitable Life Assurance Society after a scandal shook that firm. Supporters even revived talk of him running again for president in 1904; Cleveland enjoyed worrying the supporters of William Jennings Bryan, but did not seriously consider running again. Two terms, Cleveland apparently felt, had provided enough time in the White House spotlight.

13

George Clooney

Actor

*S*ome might say that George Clooney inherited more than his good looks and talent from his famous family, some may say he inherited the luck of the Irish. But they would be wrong because Clooney's rise to fame had little to do with fame.

Clooney grew up watching his father on T.V. in black and white and listening to his Aunt croon on the radio. As a small child Clooney was puzzled to see his father sitting in the same room while his face was on the T.V. Later as his father bounced from job to job and the family went from living in a mansion to living in a trailer, Clooney shied away from the gleam of stardom on T.V.

Instead Clooney took up baseball as a teenager and even tried out for his hometown Cincinnati Reds. Though he could hit the ball out of the park, Clooney lacked speed and fielding talent and was ultimately cut from the team. He then went to college and admittedly majored in "booze." After three years at school he was still a freshman and decided to go to Hollywood and live with his aunt Rosemary and her husband. He was 21 years-old.

It did not take long after that for the acting bug to bit him. His cousin, Rosemary's son, was acting in a film and that was all it took. Clooney was kicked out of his aunt's house after a year and moved in with a friend, living in his friend's walk-in closet. Clooney work odd jobs and did construction while going to one cattle-call a week. By the mid-80's Clooney had nothing in the bank, no SAG card and was riding a bike to casting calls.

25

Clooney landed an audition with ABC's head of casting, John Crosby. The audition was supposed to be done without props, but Clooney knew he was nearing the ninth inning with two guys out, nobody on and two strikes against him so he went for the fence. He decided to do a scene form Brighton Beach Memoirs which called for bunk beds so he had a couple friends bring in and set up bunk beds in a mater of 30 seconds. He did the scene and Crosby signed Clooney to ABC by the end of the day.

Clooney stumbled through "some really bad T.V.," suffered a bleeding ulcer and married and divorced actress Talia Balsam before he landed with NBC. In the late 80s Clooney did some "B" movies and landed a regular role on the sitcom The Facts of Life. He soon quit the show and worked on Roseanne before staring opposite Sela Ward on NBC's Sisters.

That is when a friend in casting slipped Clooney the pilot to ER months before anyone else saw the script. Clooney said the part of the womanizing pediatrician, Doug Ross was made for him and told executive producer, John Wells the same thing. A year later the show is a break-out hit and Clooney has a five year contract.

Clooney suffered some bumps on the way up as well. His beloved Uncle George, for which he is named, died in his arms of lung cancer at the age of 64. "My uncle said to me as he was dying 'what a waste,'" Clooney told Premiere magazine. "I remember thinking that if I die tomorrow I don't want to think what a waste."

During the second season of filming on ER, Clooney began to film his first legit motion picture, From Dusk Till Dawn, written by Quentin Tarantino. Though the movie wasn't a large commercial success Clooney's ability to make the film and shot ER paved the way for his co-stars to take on movie rolls at the same time.

Clooney's next acting Coup came when Val Kilmer bailed from the bat mobile for the Batman sequel Batman and Robin. Clooney stepped into the batsuit, co-starring with Chris O'Donnell. He also made a sleepy romantic comedy with Michelle Pfiffer, entitled One Fine Day. None of his movies however scored big at the box office. Clooney's latest effort at the box office, this summer's Out of Sight, played bettered and solidified Clooney's presence in the movies.

Clooney signed a one year contract for ER when his original contract expired and he announced that the 1998-99 season was his last as a regular on the hit show.

14

George M. Cohan

Legendary Composer

"We should make a movie with Jim (Cagney) playing the damnedest patriotic man in the country" - Jack Warner, head of Warner Bros. studios regarding George M. Cohan and the movie Yankee Doodle Dandy.

I n 1940, a grand jury investigating communist activities in America released findings that actor James Cagney was linked to red activities in the States. In an effort by movie studio executives to clear his name, the movie Yankee Doodle Dandy was made as a tribute to the life of George M. Cohan.

From Irish decent, Cohan is an Americanization of the name Keohane. But the man was just as American as he was Irish. Born in Rhode Island on the Fourth of July, two years after the nation's Centennial, Cohan grew up in a vaudeville family with the nation being his hometown. The theater was his home. To him, a dressing room was the same as a bedroom. His musical career was lauded in a musical by Catholic University in 1939.

The film goes a little further beyond Cagney and communism. First, Cohan hadn't landed a hit on Broadway since 1928. Secondly, America, on the heels of war, needed a propaganda picture to pick them up. In April of 1941, some eight months before America's entrance into World War II, Cohan signed a deal giving him full control over a movie using his music and starring Cagney. The punch line of this movie is that not throughout any part of the development or production of the film did Cagney or Cohan ever meet.

Cohan was truly a landmark figure in Hollywood. Dubbed "the First Actor" for his patriotic love for the nation, he was not only a song and dance man, but an accomplished actor. But, he was also a protective father, one of the few compliments that can be paid towards his family life. Where his father brought the children onto the set of a movie, Cohan kept his children away from movie studios. On the same note, Cohan was so involved with his work, that it took much time away from his family. He was a young man who reaped from the opportunity presented. He was a noted songwriter as a teenager and an established Broadway man at 26. He oversaw all parts of his work, from casting and producing, to composing and acting.

While Cohan is marked in the class of composers with Berlin, Rodgers, Hart and Hammerstein, but had an entirely different personality. He is remembered as a colorful character, never short of a comment or a wisecrack. He is also known as a perfectionist; a person who ran his own ship and operated in his own style. Cohan was a workaholic who never relaxed. At the end of the movie, Cagney, as Cohan, was seen lounging on a hammock, wallowing in his accomplishments. In an article from the July 1997 edition of American Heritage, his daughter remarked, "That's the kind of life Daddy would have liked to have lived."

In 1942 when the film was released, he cajoled his nurse to take him to Broadway to see the movie. He stayed for a few minutes before leaving. The trip ended up being his final jaunt to Broadway, as he died a few months later.

15

Maureen Connolly

Tennis Player

A fter being involved in an accident that ended a person's career, he or she would be forgiven if they cursed their luck.

Maureen Connolly, was no such person.

"I am lucky that the accident was not worse," she said after she was hit by a truck while riding her favorite horse. Her right leg was severely damaged, ending her pro tennis career.

And what a career it was.

"Little Mo" as the nation affectionately called her, was the first women to win the Grand Slam, claiming the Australian Open, French Open, Wimbeldon and U.S. Open in the same year, 1953. In 1951, she became the then-youngest women ever to win the U.S. open, defeating favored Shirley Fry 6-3, 1-6, 6-4. She won the next two U.S. Opens as well three straight Wimbledon singles titles, from 1952-54.

Ever since she began playing competitive tennis in her native San Diego, Little Mo was known for her dogged perseverance. No one ever heard her say "I can't do that." She survived a series of allergies in her teens to continue playing under the tutelage of Harper H. Ink, a retired businessman from Ohio who helped a number of young tennis players in the San Diego area.

Connolly was discovered by Daisy Tree, a leading tennis

player/enthusiast in the area while practicing in Griffith Park in Los Angeles. Tree referred Connolly to Teach Tennant, another well-known teacher, who became Connolly's mentor. In 1949, Tree took Connolly East to compete in the national girls' championship in Philadelphia.

And what a debut it was.

Little Mo became the darling of the tennis world after sweeping though the championships, defeating highly-touted prospect Laura Lou Jahn in straight sets. The next year, she won the Pennsylvania title, upsetting favored Helen Perez. She also defended her national girls' title, defeating Jahn again. This set the stage for the magical 1951, when she took the tennis world hostage, not letting it up until the accident of 1954.

The fact that her career ended at its peak or that she died of cancer when she was a mere 34 years old could be viewed as a tragedy. However, Connolly created a legacy of talent on the court and a combination of style, flair and dignity on and off the court that can still be felt to day. She also set the stage for Althea Gibson, Billy Jean King and the next generation of women's tennis stars who pushed the game into the modern era. Martina Navratilova, Steffi Graf and Martina Hingis today all exhibit influence of Little Mo Connolly's legacy.

And what a legacy it is.

16

Pat Conroy

Novelist

Like many novelists, much of Pat Conroy's inspiration--and stories--emanates from his own life and the life of his family. His phenomenal best-seller, "The Prince of Tides," which was later made into a major motion picture by (and starring) Barbara Streisand, found some basis in Conroy's own experiences.

Conroy had an unusual path to his literary celebrity, but, upon analysis, it becomes evident that the tapestry of his life prepared him well for his writing career. The son of an unabashedly strict disciplinarian and a mother who opted to ignore her husband's physical abuse of her children, Conroy has been open about his father's treatment of him.

He described how his father, a U.S. Marine Corps fighter pilot, would lift him up against the wall by his throat, an experience he likened to a lynching. Conroy was equally frank about his mother, describing her as "...a belle, an imagined, belle. She was poor white trash who spent her whole life denying it as bitterly and vehemently as she could..."

Conroy often depicts his family--flaws and all--in his writings, but also draws upon the more intimate details of his life, including his tribulations and the insecurities he experienced as a result of his upbringing and the fact that by the age of 15, he had lived at 23 different addresses and attended more than 11 different schools.

He found the home he yearned for in 1960 in Beaufort, South Carolina, a move that provided much of the rich life experience that would color his later writings. At Beaufort, Conroy flourished, starring on the basketball team and being given the first inkling by an English teacher that he had potential as a writer.

True to the expectations of his father, Conroy attended The Citadel, a military academy with a strict discipline policy. During one phone conversation with his mother, he lamented that life there was harsher than life with his father. His father, listening on the extension, told him he had to remain at the academy or risk being stigmatized by him for life.

Conroy's professional career began in education, when he taught at his high school alma mater, where black students were just being integrated. He left that stage to teach disadvantaged black children in a two-room schoolhouse in Daufuskie Island, South Carolina. He soon discovered that some of his students didn't even know the alphabet, let alone have the capacity to read. Further, they had little concept of the world around them.

Abandoning the traditional curriculum, he embarked on a non-traditional path, delivering oral histories and taking the children on field trips. He was fired for departing from that curriculum, but the embarrassment that jettisoning caused prompted him to begin writing with fervor.

The results, of course, are obvious. The fired school teacher has gone on to become one of the most compelling--and most candid--novelists of our time, baring his and his family's soul, sharing intimate experiences and leaving readers yearning for his next work.

The life of Pat Conroy is proof positive that fate--indeed some would say God--certainly does play a large role in our futures and all turns of event, no matter how negative they may be perceived at the time.

17

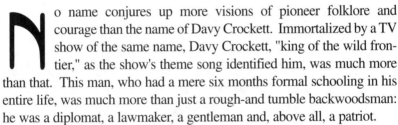

Davy Crockett

American Pioneer

No name conjures up more visions of pioneer folklore and courage than the name of Davy Crockett. Immortalized by a TV show of the same name, Davy Crockett, "king of the wild frontier," as the show's theme song identified him, was much more than that. This man, who had a mere six months formal schooling in his entire life, was much more than just a rough-and tumble backwoodsman: he was a diplomat, a lawmaker, a gentleman and, above all, a patriot.

He lived his life by a simple motto-"Be always sure you are right, then go ahead"-and those words served him well throughout his time on earth. His life is summarized by the inscription on his tombstone: Davy Crockett, Pioneer, Patriot, Solider, Trapper, Explorer, State Legislator, Congressman, Martyred at the Alamo. 1786-1836."

Crockett was all that and more. He was born on August 17, 1786, near Limestone, Tenn., in a small cabin on the shores of the Nolichucky River, the fifth of nine children of John and Rebecca Hawkins Crockett. Shortly after his birth, Crockett was moved by his family to Cove Creek in Green County, Tenn., where his father built a mill with a partner. The mill-and the Crockett home-was washed away by a flood when Davy was just eight years old. Apparently, Davy owed much of his perseverance to his father who, undeterred, moved his family to Jefferson County in Tennessee, where he constructed and ran a tavern.

When Crockett was approximately 12 years old, he got a job helping to drive cattle to Virginia. While there, he held a variety of odd jobs, returning home at the age of 15, when he took a job for men who were creditors of his father. Very early on, Crockett's skill as a marksman was apparent in local shooting competitions. He would often come away with the vaunted prize given to the best shooter-a quarter of beef-and he frequently won all four quarters of the beef given away at the competition.

His heroic efforts began as the commander of a battalion in the Creek Indian War from 1813-14. His public service continued with stints in the Tennessee legislature (1821-22 and 1823-24) and in Congress (1827-31 and 1833-35).

Despite his lack of formal education-or, perhaps, because of it-Crockett relied on his innate instincts as a leader and as a statesman. Soldiers naturally followed his, as he led by example as much as by word. One example of his combining those two was an incident during which he was pre-sented to the Governor of Tennessee and his 12-year-old daughter. Crockett took the youngster's hand and said, "When I like a man, I always love his children." Having said that, he knelt down and kissed the Governor's daughter, saying, "God bless you, my child."

Crockett perished with almost 200 other brave men at the Alamo. But even his death couldn't quell the legacy the brave frontiersman had left behind-a legacy of courage, of diplomacy and of valor.

18

Bing Crosby

Entertainer

"**B**ing" Crosby ought to be an inspiration to any young, struggling up-and-comers in showbiz. He faced more than his share of adversity, firings and career indecision before becoming one of America's favorite crooners.

Born Harry Lillis Crosby in Tacoma, Washington on May 2, 1904, he received an early introduction to music by his talented parents, especially his father, Harry. His parents moved to Spokane in 1906, where Crosby attended Gonzaga High School and received his first music lessons.

Crosby's first -- and last -- singing lesson was a flop. Already familiar with the popular music of the time courtesy of his parents' phonograph, he wanted to dispense of breathing exercises and learn how to sing the pop songs right away. While he gained little from actual vocal lessons, he would later benefit from the elocution and diction lessons he took at the high school.

He busied himself with the normal occupations of adolescent boys: basketball, baseball, and working odd jobs. He delivered papers, worked on farms and lumber camps and finally had a job he truly relished as an assistant in the prop department of the Auditorium Theatre -- his first brush with the entertainment industry.

Crosby enrolled in Gonzaga University in 1921 and joined a local music group called the Musicaladers. the band played local parties and dances until Crosby, who sang and played drums, and pianist Al Rinker were hired by a Spokane movie theater to carry the show on themselves. The next year Crosby diverged from music and studied law, taking a part time job at a local law firm. In 1925, he came to his senses and hit the road for Los Angeles with Rinker.

The duo found work in a theater, switching their act to the Metropolitan Theater two years later. It was here that Paul Whiteman found them and hired them for his band. They traveled to Chicago with Whiteman and were received well by the midwest audiences.

As the show headed east to New York, though, the duo was less of a hit. Whiteman subsequently axed them from the lineup.

Crosby went on to form the Rhythm Boys with Rinker. After the group found success, Whiteman again signed them on for a tour of the U.S. In 1930 they returned to Hollywood to make the famous film, The King Of Jazz. That film was followed by another tour of the west coast with Whiteman.

In Seattle, Crosby was canned by Whiteman again, this time for not having a "sufficiently serious attitude about his work."

He took his trio back to L.A. and found success. Crosby sang over the airwaves for the first time during an engagement with Gus Arnheim's orchestra.

It was at this juncture in his career that Crosby's star took off. he got married, did work for Mack Sennett, signed a lucrative contract with Paramount Pictures and made many successful films.

Two years later, in 1934, he cut a deal with Decca Records and honed his vocal style under Jack Kapp.

Crosby made his long-overdue first television appearance in June 1952 with his longtime colleague Bob Hope, cementing himself into the pantheon of entertainment all-time legends.

19

John Cusack

Actor

Y ou might say that John Cusack was born to be an actor.
His father, Richard Cusack, was an actor, his older sister,
Joan Cusack, a comedic actress, and his mother participated in the theatre.

With that as a lineage, it's no wonder that Cusack entered the family business of acting at the tender age of 8, working with the Evanston's Pilvan Theatre Workshop in Illinois, where his work was noticed and he went on to several jobs as a voice-over specialists.

But Cusack wasn't long for limiting his career to mere voice-overs. He was destined for the big screen, and he made that debut in the 1983 movie Class. He followed that with an appearance in 1984's 16 Candles, and really became noticed in the 1985 flick, The Sure Thing.

Perhaps his breakthrough role-at least in terms of his appeal to the opposite sex-occurred in the 1989 movie, Say Anything, where he played Lloyd Dobler, an affable, but underachieving, character with whom audiences fell in love. Prior to that, he had starred in a more serious role in Eight Men Out, a film about the Chicago White Sox baseball scandal.

He played out of character as a hit man in 1997's Grosse Point Blank, and followed that role with an equally impressive performance as Nelson Rockefeller in Cradle Will Rock in 1999.

If there is a calling card to John Cusack as an actor, it is his versatility; certainly, his ability to be chameleon-like in his portrayal of wildly different characters is one of the charms that endears him to his legion of fans. One of his landmark performances was in the Spike Jones' film, Being John Malkovich, where Cusack played a puppeteer who was able to enter Malkovich's mind. In 2002, he worked again with Jones, this time in the movie Adaptation.

Another example of the versatility of Cusack's talent is evident in the movie High Fidelity. Not only did Cusack star in the movie, he also co-wrote its script. Interestingly, the movie earned him some of his best acting reviews, as Cusack continued to mature in his craft.

It's apparent that versatility will continue to be Cusack's legacy, and that means his fans will always be anxious for the next John Cusack performance, because he dares to stretch his talents and try new and different roles each time he commits himself to a movie.

20

Dorothy Day
Journalist, Social Activist

Dorothy Day laughed it off when people called her a saint.

"When they say you are a saint," she once told an interviewer, "what they mean is that you are not to be taken seriously."

But few ever failed to take Miss Day seriously. In her 83 years of life, she discovered ways to blend her social activism with a Catholic faith that only deepened over time.

The Catholic Worker, the movement she cofounded with Peter Maurin, began with a newspaper that highlighted social programs available through the Church. Over time, needy people reached out to the Catholic Worker staff for help, and they responded by developing places to offer housing, food and clothing. The result became St. Joseph's House of Hospitality and grew gradually into a network of homes related directly and indirectly to the original.

Miss Day, a native of New York City, became interested in religion as a teenager. She originally entered the Episcopal Church. In college, however, she found it increasingly difficult to reconcile her faith with a building passion for social justice.

"I felt my faith had nothing in common with that of Christians around me," she explained in one of her books. "So I hardened my heart."

That hardness of heart only extended to religion, however. After two years at the university, she began working at the Socialist Call and joined the International Workers of the World, starting a life-long commitment to organized labor.

She left journalism for a time during World War I, becoming a nurse at a Brooklyn hospital. After the war, she spent a year in Europe, writing a novel that drew little interest, before returning to the United States and work with newspapers.

But she had not left religion behind. When she and her common-law husband, Forster Batterham, had a daughter, she decided she wanted her child to be a Roman Catholic, and Tamar Teresa was baptized.

Tamar's mother was slower to follow her daughter into the church. Batterham was a committed atheist and Miss Day felt, in her own words, that to "become a Catholic meant for me to give up a mate with whom I was very much in love." Gradually, however, the pull of faith was stronger and she was baptized into the Church.

That split between her radicalism and her Church continued for her first several years in her new faith. That changed when she met Maurin and the two opened the Catholic Worker.

Over the years, the Catholic Worker maintained its strong commitment to positions such as pacifism, a stand that cost it support during World War II. Occasionally the paper also collided with the Church itself, as when it took sides with the gravediggers against the Roman Catholic Archdiocese of New York in a Catholic cemetery strike. Miss Day stressed often, however, that faced with the choice of silence or leaving the Catholic church, she would choose silence.

Over the years, Miss Day also wrote several books and spoke often throughout the United States. She continued her commitment to causes such as racial justice and disarmament throughout her life.

21

Phil Donahue

Television Personality

P hil Donahue had a magnificent reign as a hero to housewives across the nation with his witty, cerebral talk show; a program that spoke directly to them.

"He's every wife's replacement for the husband who doesn't talk to her," remarked humorist Erma Bombeck in 1979. "They've always got Phil who will listen and take them seriously."

Indeed, Donahue has always taken his audience seriously, to the point of revolutionizing the concept of daytime talk shows. He was the first to entertain questions from the studio audience, a practice that is commonplace in today's myriad of talk shows.

The gregarious host got his humble start in Cleveland, Ohio, where he was born in 1935. After completing his education at Notre Dame University, he began working as a summer replacement at KYW-AM-TV, which he found to be "very, very boring."

In 1957, he followed his sweetheart to Albuquerque, N.M. where he took another shot at substitute announcing at KYW-TV. Disgruntled, he took a job at a local bank before hearing of an opportunity at a 250- watt radio station in Michigan. Donahue took a job as WAB's news director, where he busied himself chasing stories.

The very next year, Dayton, Ohio's WHIO-AM-TV hired him to do the half-hourly morning radio news. It was here that Donahue honed his considerable interviewing skills. His tenacity netted him interviews with such elusive figures as Jimmy Hoffa -- an interview that was later broadcast nationally by CBS.

By the mid-1960s, Donahue was producing and moderating Conversation Piece five days a week, in addition to anchoring nightly 6 and 11 p.m. newscasts. Surprisingly, he grew frustrated by his inability to catch on in a major market and walked away from his jobs to take a job as a salesman.

That career path lasted only four months, and on November 6, 1967, the determined Donahue returned to television to host a new morning show, The Phil Donahue Show. While the job was back in Dayton -- not a major market -- the interviewer was comfortable with the form. It was while hosting this show Donahue changed the face of talk TV.

"Two or three shows in, I realized the audience was asking some very good questions during commercials," Donahue told Broadcasting magazine. One day, he decided to jump out of his chair and walk into the audience to let a woman stand up and ask a question.

The boyish host endeared himself to woman almost immediately. Not only did he offer a refuge from trashy soaps and game shows, he addressed issues that concerned women: religion, consumer advocacy, sexual issues, natural childbirth, and more.

From there, he would move his act to Chicago's WGN-TV and shorten the name to Donahue. By 1974, he was picked up in other major markets and by 1980 he was on more than 200 stations. At his prime, he was watched by more than 9 million people -- about 85 percent of them women.

22

William Donovan

Diplomat, Soldier, Lawyer

William Donovan once believed he wanted to be a priest. Instead, he chose leadership in a very different kind of organization -- the World War II-era Office of Strategic Services (OSS), ancestor of the Central Intelligence Agency (CIA).

Donovan, a native of Buffalo, New York, abandoned his studies for the priesthood while in college, moving to Columbia University to complete his degree. After receiving his law degree, he returned to Buffalo to practice.

In 1912, the lawyer became a part-time soldier. Donovan joined the New York National Guard and organized Troop One of the First Calvary. During World War I, his actions earned him the Congressional Medal of Honor, the Distinguished Service Cross and the Distinguished Service Medal. Following the war, he handled several special assignments, then returned to his law practice.

Donovan ran unsuccessfully for lieutenant governor of New York before being appointed U.S. district attorney for Western New York in 1922. He moved through the ranks of the Justice Department until 1929, when he resigned to return to his law practice. Again in 1932, he unsuccessfully sought state office, this time as the candidate for governor.

43

Through the 1930s and into the 1940s, Donovan visited Europe several times, often to assess military matters. Those trips established his reputation as someone skilled in obtaining and analyzing intelligence information.

After a secret mission to Yugoslavia, Greece and the Middle East, Donovan was asked by President Franklin D. Roosevelt to create a plan for a new intelligence service. The president first named Donovan his coordinator of information, then, in 1942, chose him as director of the new OSS. That agency, an arm of the military, was charged with providing "a secret intelligence service working behind enemy lines, sabotage, morale subversion, guerrilla organization and aid to partisan resistance." For those efforts, Donovan was promoted to major general and honored by the United States and many of its allies.

Following the war, Donovan worked for a time at the Nuremberg war crimes trials before returning again to his law practice. During that period, he continued to urge creation of a permanent intelligence agency, something that finally happened with creation of the CIA. Donovan was passed over as a candidate for CIA director, but later named ambassador to Thailand in 1953. He served in that post until 1954, then returned again to his law practice.

Donovan's legacy, however, is not found in the activities of his law practice. Instead, it continues to exist to this day in the agency he encouraged the United States to create -- the CIA.

23

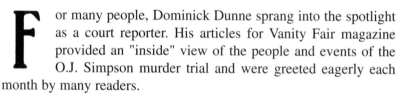

Dominick Dunne

Writer; Social Observer

F or many people, Dominick Dunne sprang into the spotlight as a court reporter. His articles for Vanity Fair magazine provided an "inside" view of the people and events of the O.J. Simpson murder trial and were greeted eagerly each month by many readers.

But Dunne had been working on highly visible projects long before 1995. The Connecticut native spent years as a television and film producer, including a stint as vice president of Four Star Television. His producing credits included the television series Adventures in Paradise and the movies The Boys in the Band and The Panic in Needle Park.

Drugs and alcohol derailed that career, however, and Dunne turned to writing. His first novel, The Winners, took characters from an earlier Joyce Haber book and moved forward with their lives. The book drew generally poor notices from critics.

For his next book, The Two Mrs. Grenvilles, Dunne began an approach he would use often, taking real events and people as a springboard for his story. Dunne based The Two Mrs. Grenvilles on a 1955 murder case. This time, some reviewers were impressed; the Los Angeles Times called it a "fast and enjoyable piece of reading."

Dunne began covering trials with one of immense personal interest -- the trial of the accused murderer of his daughter Dominique. His stories on the trial appeared both in Vanity Fair and a 1986 collection, Fatal Charms, and Other Tales of Today. The latter also featured some of Dunne's other Vanity Fair work, including celebrity profiles one reviewer called "slyly irreverent."

His third novel, People Like Us, also drew from the events surrounding the death of his daughter. While many reviewers liked the book, at least one criticized Dunne for drawing his plot from his daughter's murder. Another novel based on real events, An Inconvenient Woman, drew much more praise from reviewers.

Another collection of Vanity Fair pieces, again including celebrity profiles, appeared in 1991 under the title The Mansion of Limbo. Dunne then swung back to fiction inspired by real life, producing A Season in Purgatory in 1993. As with three of the earlier novels, A Season in Purgatory was adapted by Dunne for a television miniseries.

His court coverage for Vanity Fair continued, first with the trial of the Menendez brothers and later with the Simpson case. The Simpson case later became the basis for a novel, Another City, Not My Own.

Dunne seems able to make many cities his own, with his observations of slices of American life. With his work growing in critical and reader acceptance, it seems likely he will have more opportunities to observe those slices of life and write about them in years to come.

24

John Gregory Dunne
Novelist, Journalist, Screenwriter

Grabbing hold of predicaments that he found profoundly difficult as a youth, John Dunne developed a style and vision
unique in 20th century literature.

Born May 25, 1932 in Frog Hollow, the so-called "Irish ghet-
to" of Hartford, CT, Dunne would have a difficult time of things for
much of his adolescence. He was plagued both by his lowly station in
life and an embarrassing stuttering problem. Both of these burdens
would serve to enrich his writing with a raw and visceral truth that
emboldened his semi-autobiographic works.

Not fond of speaking out loud in class, the young Dunne concentrated his expressive energies on paper. He also paid keen attention to
the speech of others, hoping to mimic it. This served him well years
later when he wove very real dialogue into his novels and articles.

Dunne attended Catholic prep school in Rhode Island and continued his studies at Princeton University. Upon receiving his B.A. in 1954,
he joined the United States Army for a few years. Upon completing his
military stint Dunne took up residence in New York City, where he soon
caught on as a staff writer for the news magazine Time.

It was also in New York that Dunne would meet the woman he
would marry, the writer Joan Didion. He would spend the next 15 years
attempting to crawl out from under her literary shadow, finally succeeding with his 1974 novel Vegas.

After a five year romance in the city, the couple married and tentatively headed out west to California. Dunne fell in love with the west, and the two set up shop in Los Angeles to make their livings as free-lance writers.

The first to break through with a great piece of work was Didion, who made her name with the 1968 collection Slouching Towards Bethlehem. For his part, Dunne did place himself in the national spotlight for his Saturday Evening Post article on the Chicano grape-pickers' strike in Delano, California. The subject would be the basis of his first book; a book warmly received for its warmth, empathy and realism.

Dunne's second book, The Studio, was a detailed investigation into the inner workings of a major motion-picture studio. Again, critics raved about the realism; especially in regard to the lively and specific dialogue.

Random House commissioned him to write a similar book about Las Vegas, but Dunne found himself in the throes of a 17-month-long writer's block, an experience Dunne would ultimately weave into the very heart of the 1974 release, Vegas. The book blurred the lines between nonfiction, which the publisher wanted, and the touches of autobiography that were clearly present. As such he found himself among the pioneers of the "literary journalism" style that shunned objectivity but were basically works of nonfiction.

Dunne and Didion were meanwhile finding success with a number of screenplays, including the Cannes Film Festival award-winning Panic in Needle Park [1971]. While the screenplays finally brought the couple financial comfort, Dunne concentrated on his third book.

True Confessions [1977] was the book that Dunne broke through with. It drew intimately from his torturous childhood and wove in elements that were, to some, all too graphic and real. While some critics called the book focusing on the imperfections of man "gratuitous and grim," most called it provocative and full of energy. It would sell over 1 million copies and become a United Artists film starring Robert Duvall and Robert De Niro.

Dunne would continue to draw heavily from his own Irish-American heritage in his writing -- a far cry from the shame with which he wore that same heritage years before.

25

Eileen Farrell
Singer

Being the product of her vaudeville performing parents, perhaps it was natural that Eileen Farrell was to run off to New York City to explore a career in the arts. It was her own artistic graces, however, that launched her stellar career as the preeminent soprano of her day.

Born in Willimantic, Connecticut on February 13, 1920, Eileen would leave her home town and parents John and Catherine -- known professionally as "The Singing O'Farrells" -- upon completing high school. She attended art school upon arrival in New York, but soon forewent it for intensive vocal training with the former Metropolitan Opera contralto Merle Alcock. After five years of difficult tutelage under the stern Ms. Alcock, Eileen was taken under the wing of Eleanor McLellan, the teacher who would bring out the singer's genius.

Her first hint of success came in 1940 when the young talent was made a member of CBS' radio choruses and ensembles. She paid her dues and was soon given her own weekly half-hour show, Eileen Farrell Sings. This show would contribute to her diversity as a vocalist; the songs she performed ranged from operatic arias and art songs to the popular tunes of the day.

In 1947, Eileen took her show on the road, touring the United States extensively. She followed that tour up with an extended stint throughout South America.

Finally, in the fall of 1950, Eileen made her debut at New York's Carnegie Hall to rave reviews. Critics proclaimed her the most important concert star to emerge after World War II. Unfazed by her new super-stardom, she set a record during the 1950-1951 season by making 61 appearances with the New York Philharmonic.

The honors continued to pile up as the heavyweights of symphonic music took notice of Eileen and enlisted her services. Arturo Toscanini chose her as a soloist in a performance of Beethoven's Symphony No. 9 broadcast by NBC. In April of 1960, Leonard Bernstein conducted her and the New York Philharmonic-Symphony Orchestra for four performances of Beethoven's Missa Solemnis.

While dazzling high society, Eileen also expressed her love for the more contemporary popular music of the day. She made guest appearances on many television shows, debuting on the Milton Berle Show in 1950.

Eileen thoroughly dove into opera with Cherubini's Medea in 1955. She has since made many appearances in other operatic roles, touring Europe's opera houses in the late 1950s.
Despite being a Staten Island resident, Farrell did not make her debut at the Metropolitan Opera House until 1960 -- finally cementing her legitimacy as a vocal phenomenon with the few remaining skeptical critics.

Eileen was married to retired Manhattan police officer Robert Reagan on April 4, 1946. They have two children, Robert and Kathleen. In what may be a stark contrast to the diva's glamorous performances, she grew accustomed to relaxing from her busy touring and recording schedule by camping, watching boxing matches and westerns on television, knitting and doing housework -- much as any woman raised in small town Connecticut might.

26

James J. Farrell

Author

Critics either love or hate the feisty naturalism of James Farrell. Those that love him praise his gritty contributions to social realism, while those that try to dismiss his work as indecent and vulgar find they cannot.

Such is the influence of the chronicler of Chicago's former Irish South Side. Farrell was born in the working class neighborhood on Feb. 27, 1904 and raised by his grandmother and uncle. It was here Farrell cut his teeth in his first saloons, pool halls and athletic fields. His rough and tumble upbringing would be instrumental in nearly all his loosely labeled works of "fiction," and provide the backdrop for his O'Neill saga, Lonigan books and other writings.

Farrell does not reflect fondly upon his childhood, where he involved himself in rough and tumble activities, most respectably on the baseball diamond. At St. Cyril High School -- while not distinguishing himself academically -- he earned letters in baseball, football and basketball.

He escaped the South Side to attend the University of Chicago where he took to an inspiring English professor. He became a voracious reader and decided to become a writer.

At the age of 28, his first novel, Young Lonigan; A Boyhood in Chicago Streets was published specifically for and limited to readers "having a professional interest in the psychology of adolescence." Critics called it an instant classic, but decided it was called a novel for lack of a better term. While they said it read more like a case history, they felt the young writer was worth keeping an eye upon.

Farrell continued to divide the press in his next two novels Gas-House Mcginty [1934] and The Young Manhood of Studs Lonigan. Some said he was out simply for shock value, while others thought the stark realism was genuine, honest and heart-felt.

Farrell brought the Lonigan trilogy to a conclusion with 1935's Judgment Day and, before continuing with his next series, wrote the non-fiction piece A Note in Literary Criticism. That same year he won a Guggenheim Fellowship in creative writing to launch a new series.

The fist book was A World I Never Made [1936], which still focused on the Irish in Chicago. Protagonist Danny O'Neill was less than the prototypical hero, but again, sincere. This novel ruffled more feathers than any of the others: The New York Times refused to accept advertisements for it, libraries pulled it off their shelves and special interest groups flocked to point out "indecent passages."

Courts threw the case out after prominent writers and critics flocked to Farrell's defense. The Book-of-the-Month Club subsequently granted Farrell one of their four $2,500 prizes for "the strong and vigorous sincerity with which he represents an underprivileged section of American life."

Farrell has never been one to compromise his style for social acceptance or marketability. He has been quoted as counseling young authors to "forget about the market and the element of commerce in literature" and write honestly and truthfully about what they know best.

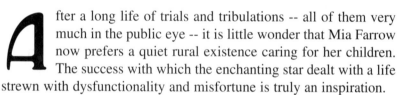

27

Mia Farrow

Actress

After a long life of trials and tribulations -- all of them very much in the public eye -- it is little wonder that Mia Farrow now prefers a quiet rural existence caring for her children. The success with which the enchanting star dealt with a life strewn with dysfunctionality and misfortune is truly an inspiration.

Her ups and downs began at an early age. Farrow was born of actress Maureen O'Sullivan and film director John Farrow. She grew up in Beverly Hills with her parents. At the tender age of nine, Farrow contracted polio and had to be quarantined from her own family. While she was in a ward with other children suffering from the disease, she could see her parents -- behind glass -- twice a week.

It was at this time, Farrow has said, she developed the toughness and coping mechanisms that would serve her well later in life. Farrow's father moved the family to Spain to film a movie when she was 12. The very next year, 1957, Farrow's brother Michael was killed in a plane crash. Close on the heels of that tragedy the patriarch of the Farrow family died of a heart attack.

While her father had always discouraged Farrow from entering the entertainment industry, the family had no money after his death. The young actress took a role on television's first evening drama, Peyton's Place.

That role led to her marriage to her first boyfriend, the much older Frank Sinatra. While he also forbade her from acting, she decided to take a role in Roman Polanski's 1967 film Rosemary's Baby. While on the set, she received word that Sinatra had filed for divorce.

Three years later Farrow took marriage vows again, this time with conductor André Previn. Their marriage produced three children but failed in 1979, and it was only a few years before she struck up a romance with quirky writer/director/actor Woody Allen.

Perhaps more cautious, she never married Allen and kept a separate apartment during their 12-year relationship. They had one child together and adopted several more.

Their tumultuous love and film relationship received its share of media scrutiny, culminating in their break-up earlier this decade. Allen's well-documented romance with Soon-Yi Previn -- Farrow's adopted daughter -- was another painful episode for the actress.

Her resolve held. She detached herself from the Hollywood glitz and games, choosing a more settled existence in Connecticut with her children. The mother of 12 devotes herself to other affairs now. She wrote an autobiography and spends quiet evenings at home, preferring the reassuring comfort of "tucking my children in at night to going out to a concert or having dinner."

28

F. Scott Fitzgerald
Author

H is four novels were never contemporary best-sellers, but he is truly considered today to be one of the greatest American writers of all time. F. Scott Fitzgerald fought alcohol, his wife's schizophrenia, financial woes--and his own genius-- in a career that was far too short and left so much yet to be written.

He is considered to be the writer most closely associated with the 1920s, so much so that the title he imparted on that decade--the Jazz Age--became its unofficial moniker.

Fitzgerald broke on to the literary scene in 1920 with "This Side of Paradise," a novel set at Princeton--where he attended, but never completed--that is considered to be the definitive study of the post-war generation's sense of values.

His crowning literary achievement was "The Great Gatsby," recent-ly ranked as the second-greatest book written in the 20th century. That work, which studied the life, times and travails of Jay Gatsby, is considered the quintessential work on the American dream. Fitzgerald wrote that novel while in France, away from the tumult of New York City.

Alas, Fitzgerald's own dream of concentrating primarily on novels never materialized. Because his books, though well-received by critics, did not sell extraordinarily well, Fitzgerald found himself time and time again opting to write short stories for magazines in order to maintain financial stability. Fitzgerald, never one to curb a lifestyle as extravagant as was his talent, became known during his time as a writer of stories rather than as a writer of novels. Indeed, he wrote some 160 of those stories, earning at his peak in 1929 a fee of $4,000 per story from The Saturday Evening Post. And Fitzgerald had a sense that his writing was important and, perhaps, enduring.

In fact, he once wrote his daughter: "I am not a great man, but sometimes I think the impersonal and objective quality of my talent, and the sacrifices of it, in pieces, to preserve its essential value has some sort of epic grandeur."

Certainly, there were sacrifices along the way. Work on another classic, "Tender is the Night," stagnated when his wife, Zelda, experienced a schizophrenic breakdown. Needing money, he again turned to the less-literary but more-financially rewarding story writing in order to pay for his wife's expense--and, alas, somewhat ineffective--treatments.

When Americans' interest in short fiction ebbed and that market drying up for Fitzgerald, he tried his hand , with limited success, at screenwriting. That experience helped him to write "The Love of the Last Tycoon," a novel about Hollywood still judged as one of the greatest ever written. He died while writing that novel, which was published posthumously in 1941.

Fitzgerald's immense talents have endured more than a half-century beyond his death and will continue to endure forever. His mastery of writing, his uncanny character depictions and his passion combined to give the world four classic novels and 160 compelling short stories.

Certainly, Fitzgerald was correct in saying that his work has "some sort of epic grandeur."

Indeed.

29

Thomas FitzSimons

Signer of the Constitution; Government Leader;

Businessman

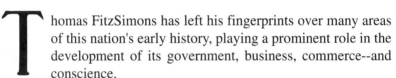

T homas FitzSimons has left his fingerprints over many areas of this nation's early history, playing a prominent role in the development of its government, business, commerce--and conscience.

Born in Ireland in 1741, FitzSimons came to America early in his youth and began a career in shipping, thanks in large part to his marriage to Catharine Meade, whose father, Robert, was a vastly successful merchant. FitzSimons joined with his brother-in-law to form George Meade & Co., which carried on substantial trade with the West Indies.

FitzSimons was an early and fervent proponent of the colonies' desire to split away from England; in fact, he organized and commanded a militia that was extremely active during the Revolutionary War. Generous with his money, FitzSimons donated 5,000 pounds near the end of the war to help the fledgling army meet its needs.

He was elected to the Constitutional Convention in 1782 and was a signer of the original Constitution. Just as importantly, FitzSimons was the loudest voice during that convention in convincing his colleagues to pay all moneys due to its soldiers, saying that debt was one of deepest obligation and honor.

57

He was elected to the first Congress and embraced the government philosophies of Alexander Hamilton, who espoused the importance of a strong federal government with broad powers to nationalize. Throughout his Congressional career, which ended with his defeat in 1794, he emphasized the need for the new country to stay debt-free--a lesson well heeded in today's time of unfathomable national debt.

His departure from office was not the end of FitzSimon's influence on early America, though it does transfer to a different sphere. He was instrumental in the establishment of the first bank of the new country--the Bank of North America, was a founder and a director of the Insurance Company of North America.

Not one to shirk civic duties, FitzSimons also served for several years as the president of the Philadelphia Chamber of Commerce, and was the largest contributor to the construction of St. Augustine's church in Philadelphia.

His most enduring contribution, however, was his insistence that the United States pay the debt it owed to its soldiers, and his belief that the country should remain debt free. His influence on early political thinking in the Untied States is evident, as are his contributions to the success of the Revolutionary War--and the success of the new country that war produced.

30

Robert Flaherty
Filmmaker

Robert Flaherty first went to northern Quebec in search of iron ore. What he eventually found there was a career as a documentary filmmaker.

That career grew, in part, from Flaherty's long-time interest in the people and resources of northern Canada. He first visited that area as a child, when he accompanied his father, a mine manager, to a job in northern Ontario.

That experience stayed with Flaherty after college. At his father's suggestion, he agreed to work for Sir William Mackenzie, who was seeking someone to look for iron ore in the remote islands of the Hudson Bay. Flaherty traveled through the Hudson and Ungava Bay coasts from 1910 to 1913, and was the first white man into some of the territory he visited. In honor of his work, the Canadian government gave his name to one of the islands in the Belcher's Islands group in Hudson Bay.

In 1913, while Flaherty was preparing for the third trip, Mackenzie suggested he take a movie camera. It was a wise suggestion -- Flaherty was stranded on Baffin Island through the winter of 1913-1914, and he spent that time making films. He shot film again during a fourth trip.

59

Flaherty intended to turn that film into a movie on Eskimo life. Before he could do so, however, his negatives were destroyed in a fire. It took him several years before he could obtain financial backing from Revillon Frères, a fur company, to return and reshoot the lost film.

The director returned to Canada with a plan to show the Eskimos' struggle for survival in a difficult environment. To bring that vision to life, he would occasionally set up scenes -- for example, he would ask his subjects to wear the traditional clothing they had abandoned.

"Sometimes you have to lie," he explained. "One often has to distort a thing to catch its true spirit."

His film, called Nanook of the North, achieved worldwide success. That success led a studio to hire Flaherty to make "another Nanook," this time in Samoa. Manoa, released in 1926, was a success in Europe, but generally received less notice in the United States. His wife's suggestion that he work with a British government agency led directly to the film Industrial Britain and indirectly to another film, Man of Aran.

Flaherty's one commercial film was Elephant Boy, a dramatization of Rudyard Kipling's Jungle Book shot in India. After that, he returned to the United States to shoot The Land and, after World War II, Louisiana Story, a film about a Cajun boy in the Louisiana bayous.

Throughout his career, Flaherty's wife, Frances, worked with him on the writing and editing of his films. Mrs. Flaherty helped him explore the areas he portrayed in his films, and shape the story he wanted to tell. But the central factor of his films was his talent, his eye for film and the ability to bring other people's lives to the screen in a way that fascinates audiences.

31

John Ford
Movie Director; Actor

A s a child, John Ford was fascinated by the movies. As an adult, Ford ended up in Hollywood, creating the kind of films that still fascinate viewers.

Ford began life in Maine, a full continent from his eventual home. He first moved to California to join his older brother, Francis, who had become successful as an actor and director. Francis promptly hired his brother for jobs ranging from acting to prop man.

John's eye for directing was quickly apparent. By the end of that first year, he was an assistant director. He moved from that to handling short films and Westerns. That experience helped him get a contract with Fox Studios to direct feature films.

Quickly, those Fox features caught the eye of the public and critics. With The Iron Horse, made in 1924, his audience expanded to include people outside the United States. The film was among the top-grossing movies of the 1920s.

The introduction of talking pictures, a career-killer for some, simply gave Ford an additional resource to tell his story. With a frequent collaborator, screenwriter Dudley Nichols, he made The Informer, a film which won him the Academy Award for direction. His 1939 film, Stagecoach, captured two Oscars and turned its featured actor, John Wayne, into a star.

Through World War II, Ford made well-regarded documentaries as chief of the Field Photographic Branch of the Office of Strategic Services. One of those, The Battle of Midway, won an Oscar for best documentary.

After the war, Ford returned to create more well-regarded films, including many Westerns. He worked so often with the Navajo Indians of Monument Valley that they inducted him into the tribe with the name Natani Nez (Tall Soldier). His last commercial film for a studio was Seven Women, in 1965.

Throughout, Ford fought to "do something fresh" with his movies, rather than fall into the Hollywood pattern. "First they want you to repeat your last picture ... Then they want you to continue whatever vein you succeeded in with the last picture." He said he had too much respect for his audience to provide them with cookie-cutter films.

Certain themes did recur in Ford's films, however. He often set his stories in the American West during the years it was being settled. His heroes were not infrequently loners who had to fight others to achieve self-respect.

Unlike some in Hollywood, Ford was honored for his work during his lifetime. Five months before his death, he received the first Life Achievement Award from the American Film Institute. At that same ceremony, he received the Medal of Freedom from President Richard Nixon.

And even after his death in 1973, his films have continued to give audiences the joy he experienced in seeing a movie.

32

Henry Ford
Automotive Pioneer

e owe much of the American way of life to the genius and inspiration of Henry Ford.

The man not only revolutionized the automotive industry, he revolutionized all of manufacturing, with his brilliant concept and implementation of the assembly line-an idea that not only increased efficiency and production, but also enhanced quality and performance.

He is a hero not only for his genius, but for his benevolence, for his philanthropy and for his the legacy he left on American industry and the American landscape. Indeed, America would be a much different country without the contributions of Henry Ford. Today, one of his legacies-the Ford Foundation-grants millions in contributions to charitable and non-profit organizations in an effort to improve the quality and integrity of life for Americans throughout the country.

Henry Ford was born in Dearborn, Michigan, in 1863, years after his parents had emigrated from Ireland in the 1840s to escape the potato famine. Like many in his time, Ford's formal education was limited, but he was gifted with an innate curiosity and an uncanny ability to build and repair machinery.

That skill landed him an early job with the Detroit Edison Company, where he rose quickly through the ranks from an apprentice to the company's lead engineer. An inveterate tinkerer, Ford in the early 1890s built his own gasoline engine and, later, his own car, a foretaste of what was to come.

Just before the turn of the century, Ford became one of the leaders of the Detroit Automobile Company. While there, he advanced the idea that cars-which were then virtually built one at a time-could be better and more quickly built using standard parts and assembly line methods. His idea was scoffed at by those in charge, so Ford left and began building his own auto racing cars. His success in that field merited enough credibility that he was able to woo people to partner and back him with his own company, founded in 1903-the Ford Motor Company.

By 1908, he had begun mass production of the famed Model T, and by 1913, he had implemented the first moving assembly line. Manufacturing was never to be the same. By the time Ford stopped production of the Model T in 1927, more than 15 million of the cars had been sold.

While accomplishing all of this, Ford also increased the pay given to his employees and, at the same time, decreased their work hours. Ford's contributions to manufacturing and labor are the stuff of legend, and his influence continues to this very day.

He toyed with another love of his-politics-and ran unsuccessfully for Senate on the Democratic ticket. Though he remained active in politics and was frequently called on to advise leaders on governmental and business affairs, he never again ran for office, preferring to use his influence in more private circles.

He died in 1947, leaving behind a powerful automobile empire but, more importantly, leaving behind a legacy of innovation and genius that still has impact today.

33

Jackie Gleason
Comedian, TV star

One of the most telling tests of greatness for a performer is that he or she is known simply by a nickname. It's by no accident that Jackie Gleason is known, and will be known for ages, as simply, "The Great One."

Jackie Gleason's "The Honeymooners" is a defining show in TV history; it was the first truly successful TV ensemble program and remains today as a landmark in the legacy of comedy on television, gaining new audiences in reruns more than four decades after it had concluded its CBS run.

Though he starred in numerous films and TV shows, Jackie Gleason will always be remembered as Ralph Cramden, the lovable bus driver who was constantly getting into and out of jams with his wife, Alice, and his best friend, Ed Norton.

The simplicity of the show's set--usually Cramden's kitchen--allowed full focus to be given to Gleason's enormous comedic talents and his impeccable comedic timing. With Norton, Alice and Trixie as the perfect set-ups and foils, Cramden never failed to draw laughter and sympathy from audiences as Gleason played the character for all the laughs and understanding only a great one like he could wring from the portrayal.

65

Despite its short run, The Honeymooners remains today as a comedy classic, mentioned in the same breath as "I Love Lucy," "The Dick Van Dyke Show," and "The Mary Tyler Moore Show." It was arguably the first true ensemble comedy on TV, with Gleason as the acknowledged star but with the other three members of the troupe crucial components in the show's success.

The Great One was more than just a legendary comedian, though: he could do drama with the best of them as well. His performance in the movie, "The Hustler," is still one of Hollywood's classic dark portrayals--a role for which Gleason drew from the experiences of his own background, which smacked of hard, poor times. He once said, "A buck never threw its arms around my parents," but that was the least of the young Gleason's worries. His father deserted them when he was eight and Gleason's mother and older brother both died just a few years later.

Gleason eked out a living in pool halls, giving him ample experience to draw on years later for his memorable performance in "The Hustler." His show business career began at age 15, when he won a local talent contest and got a job as a master of ceremonies for $3/night.

He made his TV debut as the title character in The Life of Riley, preceding the lovable William Bendix in that role. Following The Honeymooners, Gleason again dominated TV with his "The Jackie Gleason Show," a weekly variety program that further brought to life several of Gleason's most memorable characters.

34

William R. Grace

Mayor of New York City, entrepreneur

illiam R. Grace followed an unlikely path from his birth in County Cork, Ireland, to his becoming mayor of New York City. In between those landmark events in his life were excursions to Peru, booming businesses, poor health and a remarkable career that had an indelible impact on New York City and in Peru

Grace's first love always was the sea, and he answered that wanderlust in his heart when, as a young boy, he ran away from home and got a job on a ship bound for the United States. He spent two years in the U.S. as a clerk for mercantile house, but then reignited his affair with the sea when his father gave him an interest in a ship chandlery firm in England.

Soon afterwards, he traveled to Peru, where he and his brother organized the Grace Brothers shipping company, which quickly spread Boston, Baltimore and Liverpool, dominating the export trade from South America. This business quickly made Grace and his brother extremely wealthy, and also set the stage for more business enterprises in the future.

He returned to the United States in 1860 to tend to poor health, and began the W.R. Grace & Co shipping firm, and the Grace Steamship Co. It wasn't long before the Grace touch again surfaced, enabling him and his companies to control the carrying trade between the United States and Latin America.

His Peruvian connections served him well at this time, allowing him to secure vital business concessions and making his companies even more dominant and profitable. He became a confidant and consultant to the Peruvian government, handling most of the supply contracts for the Peruvian railroad effort and equipping the country's armed services.

In 1880, Grace became the first Roman Catholic ever to be elected Mayor of New York City, and he went right to work, making good on his campaign promises of cleaning up police corruption and organized vice. He won re-election in 1884, and, after that term was up, refocused his energies on his interests in Peru.

That country had emerged in 1883 from a costly war with Chile and had a debt so staggering that it could not pay it. Peru turned to its friend, Grace, who agreed to take over management of the national debt in exchange for mineral, land and railroad concessions.

Consequently, Grace leaves a legacy in two countries: in Peru, he is remembered for his role in helping to build the country both before and after its war with Chile; and in the United States, he leaves the heritage of not only being the first Irish-Catholic mayor of New York, but also of having the political and personal courage to fight corruption among police.

35

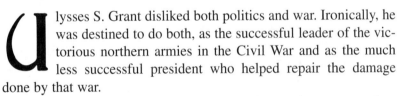

Ulysses S. Grant

General, President

U lysses S. Grant disliked both politics and war. Ironically, he was destined to do both, as the successful leader of the victorious northern armies in the Civil War and as the much less successful president who helped repair the damage done by that war.

Grant had not planned to be a soldier. His direction was set when his father, Jesse, obtained for him an appointment to West Point. As a cadet, his record, except in mathematics and horsemanship, was average. Even at graduation, he did not look forward to a military career.

He entered active duty in time to serve in the Mexican War. Although he was not a supporter of the war, he served with distinction throughout. But even promotions did not encourage thoughts of a military career.

After the war, Grant married Julia Dent. His military duties separated them early; orders sent Grant to the west coast by way of Panama, a journey considered too dangerous for family travel. On the West Coast, Grant at times buried loneliness in drink. That led to a warning from his commander; he answered by resigning.

In August of 1854, former soldier Grant joined his family in St. Louis. Over the next six years, he tried farming, real estate, politics and serving as a clerk in a custom house. He was successful at none of them. He was heading for Galena, Illinois, to join two of his brothers in a leather store, when the war broke out.

After some months, Grant was named colonel of the 21st Illinois Volunteers. As administrator of a district headquartered at Cairo, Illinois, Grant established his reputation with a well-executed maneuver that took two Southern forts and cut the rebel army in two. His victory raised spirits through the North and earned him another promotion.

Even with some defeats, Grant had earned a very important supporter, President Abraham Lincoln. Faced with one of many demands for Grant's removal as commander, Lincoln's reply was simple: "I can't spare this man. He fights."

Reports from Charles A. Dana and more field successes built Lincoln's confidence in Grant. Supporters urged him to run for president; he emphasized he wanted only to end the war. Lincoln gave him that chance, promoting him to general-in-chief. His new commander replied with a coordinated plan to end the confederacy's ability to fight.

By April 9, 1865, he had done so. That day, General Robert E. Lee surrendered on terms so considerate that he did not question them. Seventeen days later, the war was over.

Grant at first headed military demobilization efforts. However, by 1868, he agreed to be nominated for president. Although he took no active part in the campaign, he won the election.

The new president enjoyed life in the White House, but found the job far less pleasant. Critics rapped his appointments and his performance, although he moved forward in areas such as foreign policy. The criticism prompted a decision not to seek a third term.

Shortly after leaving office, he and his family fulfilled a long-held desire to tour Europe. When he returned, supporters again asked him to run for president. He refused, and moved into his difficult last few years.

Through that last period, the former president was dogged by financial and health problems. Shortly before his death, he began work on his Personal Memoirs. As with many of Grant's accomplishments, it would be more appreciated after his death -- the book became one of the most successful of that period in American history.

36

Benjamin Harrison
U.S. President, Attorney

Benjamin Harrison's interest in public affairs eventually brought him to the office of the President of the United States. But throughout his adult life, he perhaps more enjoyed his work as an attorney, and he was pleased to return to that after his presidency.

Harrison, a native of Ohio, joined many in his generation by moving further west. After studying law in Cincinnati, he and his family moved west to Indianapolis. There, he gradually acquired a good reputation both as an attorney and as a campaign speaker.

His interest in politics began early in his law practice. Discussion of slavery drew major national interest, and Harrison felt the Republicans held the moral position. By 1858, he was serving as secretary to the state Republican central committee. Later, he served as city attorney and as reporter of the supreme court of Indiana.

At the start of the Civil War, Harrison helped gather men and material for the 70th Indiana Infantry. He was rewarded for those efforts when then-Gov. Oliver P. Morton named him a colonel of the infantry. His reputation for good service continued, and by war's end, he had been promoted to brigadier general.

After the war, Harrison returned to his law practice, strengthening both his good reputation and his financial position. He continued to campaign through Indiana for Republican candidates. He managed to dodge suggestions that he himself run until 1876, when he was persuaded that his duty to his party required him to become a candidate for governor. Perhaps to his relief, the Democrats won and Harrison could again return to his law practice.

But he could not continue to dodge those who felt he would be an asset in a public post. He served as a member of the Mississippi River Commission and a citizens' committee to settle a national railroad strike; he also continued to be active in party politics. By the time Ulysses S. Grant sought the presidency, Harrison was being considered as a candidate for vice president. However, he refused to allow himself to be nominated.

He did not decline election to the United States Senate, however, serving there from 1881 to 1887. While a senator, Harrison defended the rights of settlers and Indians against the railroads and supported what he saw as fair railroad regulation. He was not re-elected.

Through the next several years, friends and supporters began a quiet campaign to have Harrison nominated for the presidency. They achieved that goal at the 1888 Republican convention. Although Grover Cleveland actually won the popular vote, Harrison took the electoral college and, with it, the presidency.

The successes through Harrison's presidency were lower-key ones, including new, more efficient practices in the post office. He also gave considerable attention to the opening of the Oklahoma Territory and new tariff laws. In part because of a split in the Republican party, however, Harrison was defeated for re-election, ironically by Grover Cleveland, the man he had defeated four years earlier.

After that defeat, Harrison once again returned to Indianapolis to practice law. He also accepted many invitations to speak. His pleasure in his work and outside interests and the joys of a new family, created by his second marriage, allowed the former president to finish his life with perhaps more joy than he ever took in holding the office of president.

37

Helen Hayes

Actress

F
ew have brought the same glow and glamour to the stage as Helen Hayes, and few have continuously succeeded in outdoing herself as the deserved "First Lady of the American Stage."

Critics and fans alike seemed to become more infatuated with Hayes every year during her long theatre, movie and radio career.

Hayes' portrayal of Queen Victoria in the Gilbert Miller production of Laurence Housman's Victoria Regina was deemed to be clearly her best performance.

"Many count Victoria Regina their happiest experience in all modern theater," critic Maxwell Anderson wrote in 1955.

For four years Hayes played the part, 969 performances in all. Each night she would age eighty years over the span of 150 minutes, a feat cherished by fans and recognized with the Drama League of New York Medal for most distinguished performance of 1936.

Spring of 1944 brought about another monumental role for Hayes, this time in the theater production Harriet. Critics called the actress' portrayal of Harriet Beecher Stowe "a masterpiece."

Critics had reason to gush again six years later when Hayes took the role of Lucy Andree Ransdell in The Wisteria Trees, a production based on Anton Chekhov's The Cherry Orchard. The New York Times called it "the richest performance of her career."

Hayes returned to a familiar role as Maggie Wylie in the New York City Center Theatre Company's revival of What Every Woman Knows in 1954. This time it was writer William Hawkins calling her effort "the triumph of a whole career."

Helen Hayes Brown was born Oct. 10, 1900 in Washington D.C. She made amateur theatrical appearances as a very young girl, joining a Washington acting company at the age of five.

By the time she turned 17 she had played New York City and, in fact, toured the whole country in the lead of Pollyanna. The very next year she hit Broadway as Margaret Schofield in Penrod.

Hayes continued a torrid pace, appearing in countless productions before meeting and marrying playwright Charles G. MacArthur in August 1928. She took a brief hiatus while pregnant with daughter Mary, but returned to the stage in 1930.

By this time, she had caught the eye of Hollywood filmmakers and launched into an equally successful film career. She received an Oscar for her role in the 1931 release The Sin of Madelon Claudet. She starred in a number of well-received movies before returning to the stage.

Amazingly, Hayes found time to do radio productions, debuting in 1930 and proceeding to do noteworthy work with Orson Wells before producing and acting in CBS' Helen Hayes Theatre, winning an award for radio's best actress for 1940.

Television work, too, followed; along with charity work. Hayes became the national chairman of the women's division of the National Foundation for Infantile Paralysis, her interest in the ailment piqued by the death of Mary in 1949. A stout republican, the diminutive actress threw her weight behind Ike as the women's chairman of the National Citizens for Eisenhower in 1956.

38

Victor Herbert

Composer and Conductor

Medicine's loss was music's gain. That, in a nutshell, summarizes the serendipity that occurred when Victor Herbert was forced to forsake a career in medicine because he and his family simply did not have the funds necessary to allow him to pursue his dream of becoming a doctor.

But music--perhaps more than medicine--was what was truly coursing through Herbert's veins. His grandfather was the celebrated Irish poet and composer Samuel Lover, and so it came as no surprise to Herbert's mother when he showed tremendous musical aptitude at a very early age.

He is best remembered for his innovation and creativity in seeing the possibilities of joining music to then-emerging use of sound on films; in fact, it is believed that his symphonic score for the film, The Fall of a Nation, may have been the first composed score for a feature film.

His talents shone most brilliantly in his favorite venue, the operetta, of which he wrote more than 40, including the acclaimed Babes in Toyland in 1903. Typical of his operettas was his belief that the listener/viewer should feel good at the end: virtually all of Herbert's works concluded on the upbeat, with right triumphing over right and with a sense of justice and happiness pervading the conclusion

Herbert's works often strained the vocal abilities of singers, because his wide-ranging compositions required singers to be extremely flexible and versatile while having a great range and pitch. But, with the right singers, his music was harmonic and powerful and a delight to hear.

Herbert is also well-remembered for changing the course of copyright history when, in 1914, he and others founded ASCAP, the nation's first and most powerful force in protecting against copyright infringement of songs and other works. Herbert had a long history of speaking out in behalf of protecting copyrights, having testified before Congress on the importance of securing composers' royalties on the sale of recorded cylinders, discs and piano rolls. To this very day, ASCAP is a watchdog against copyright infringement, and composers and musicians alike have made untold millions of royalties because of the visionary work by Herbert and others.

Herbert's life took a fateful turn after his father died when he was just an infant; his mother remarried a Germany physician, Dr. Wilhelm Schmid, and moved to Germany, where his musical talents were eventually polished and matured.

He studied music at Germany's famous Stuttgart Conservatory in two different stints, and met his wife, Therese Foerster, a soprano, while a student there. The two then emigrated from Ireland to America in 1886, answering a call from the Metropolitan Opera Company to employ his wife as a soloist and Herbert as a cellist.

Herbert not only contributed to the rich cache of music because of his compositions, he also impacted strongly on the ability of those who write music and lyrics to collect what was rightfully theirs through his work with ASCAP.

39

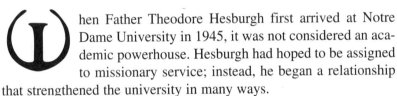

Theodore Hesburgh
Priest, Retired President of Notre Dame University

hen Father Theodore Hesburgh first arrived at Notre Dame University in 1945, it was not considered an academic powerhouse. Hesburgh had hoped to be assigned to missionary service; instead, he began a relationship that strengthened the university in many ways.

Hesburgh had known from childhood that he wanted to be a priest. He considered the Jesuit order, but in high school decided instead to become a part of the Congregation of Holy Cross, the community which established the University of Notre Dame. Hesburgh studied at Notre Dame and the Holy Cross seminary there, then obtained graduate education before returning to Notre Dame as a teacher of religion and chaplain to its war veterans.

His new positions allowed Hesburgh to gauge the feelings of Notre Dame's students. Strong advocacy for the students led to his first promotion, as he was named executive vice president in 1949.

Hesburgh accepted the post reluctantly, noting he "never wanted to be an administrator, but I have this vow of obedience." Three years later, he was again asked to be obedient, as the order named him university president.

President Hesburgh immediately began reducing the number of regulations on campus. He would not, however, eliminate nearly all rules, giving student protesters the option of accepting the remaining rules or leaving.

The new president also began strengthening the university's academic programs, introducing a new liberal arts curriculum. Working with Father Edmund Joyce Jr., his executive vice president, Hesburgh led drives that had raised $150 million by 1977. Those funds built new buildings, strengthened several programs, improved faculty salaries and allowed creation of new programs.

Those funds also prompted a change in Notre Dame governance. Citing the need for more accountability, Hesburgh led an effort that made Notre Dame the first Catholic university in the world to shift control to a primarily lay board of trustees

Increasingly during the 1960s, Hesburgh walked a careful line in two areas. He argued for the right of Notre Dame professors to discuss all points of view, distinguishing between the Church's teaching authority and the role of the Catholic university.

His best known response to student protest was a February 1969 open letter telling protesters who used force that they would be suspended or, if not students, arrested for trespass. At the same time, however, he cautioned the Nixon administration not to overreact to student disorders. Gradually, he did make some of the changes requested, including the introduction of women students.

Through most of his presidency, Hesburgh also served outside the bounds of Notre Dame. In 1957, he joined the United States Commission on Civil Rights, becoming chairman 12 years later. He served as chair of the Rockefeller Foundation board of trustees and as a member of boards including the Carnegie Commission on the Future of Higher Education and the United Negro College Fund, Chase Manhattan Bank and National Science Foundation. He also rejected some federal posts, including an offer by President Lyndon B. Johnson to head the space program.

Hesburgh retired as Notre Dame president in 1987. Before and after that time, he has received awards including the United States Medal of Freedom and more than 120 honorary degrees. But perhaps his greatest honor, and his legacy, is the recognition throughout the nation of the educational strength of the University he led for 35 years.

40

Ben Hogan
Professional Golfer

Ben Hogan didn't burst on the golfing scene as a young phenomenon -- he was into his late 20s before his first tournament win, at the Hershey Invitational. Once he started, however, Hogan was difficult to stop.

During his golfing career, he won 61 tournaments, including nine major titles. In 1953, Hogan won three of the world's top four golf tournaments, the U.S. Open, the British Open and the Masters. He won three more U.S. Opens, in 1948, 1950 and 1951; one more Masters title, in 1951; and two Professional Golfers Association (PGA) titles, in 1946 and 1948.

Other golfers and observers tried in many ways to explain how Hogan became so successful. Writer Grantland Rice explained Hogan used practice, concentration and the will to overcome his handicaps. Fellow golfer Bobby Jones offered a simpler explanation: he told a reporter that Hogan was the hardest worker at the game of anyone he'd ever seen.

That hard work became particularly important after 1949, when Hogan's career was almost ended by injuries sustained in an automobile accident. He was not ready to stop golfing, however, and fought back to become the U.S. Open champion again in 1950.

Hogan first began golfing as a shopboy at the Glen Garden Country Club in Fort Worth. He was left-handed, but golfed with a right-handed grip because he could not afford left-handed clubs as a youngster. By 1932, Hogan had become the pro at the Oakhurst, Texas, country club.

The young golfer tried tournament competition without success in 1931 and 1937. In 1938, however, he was able to find a winning rhythm, coming in second in the Professional Golfers Association tournament in Oakland, California, and first in the Hershey Invitational.

By 1940, Hogan was the tour's money-winner of the year, winning four tournaments and placing high in 19 others. From August 1939 to September 1941, he placed in the money in 56 consecutive tournaments. His 1941 record again made him the tour's top money-winner.

After a two-year break for military service, Hogan returned to professional golf in 1945, winning his third tournament with a score of 19 under par. He set a PGA record by scoring 261 for 72 holes in that year's Portland Golf Club Invitation tournament.

Once again in 1946, Hogan was the top money-winner in professional golf, with winnings of $37,877. A year later, he was also leading the American team to a win over the British in the first Ryder Cup competition in 10 years.

In 1948, Hogan became the first golfer in 26 years to win what were then the tour's three top American events -- the PGA, the National Open and the Western Open -- in the same year. He was named "golfer of the year" by a number of sports writers and by the editor of the Official Golf Guide.

In later years, Hogan was not quite as successful. Losses in the U.S. Open in 1955 and 1956 prevented him from becoming the only golfer to win the U.S. Open five times. Those misses, however, have not prevented golfers since then from remembering and honoring Hogan for his impressive achievements in his sport.

41

John Philip Holland
Inventor

J ohn Philip Holland's notion that a boat could be submerged and become an effective weapon in war--as well as an important instrument in science and exploration--was greeted with dubious indignity virtually every time he espoused it as a young man. Indeed, though some others had failed in designing a practical submarine before him--and many of his own efforts also failed--Holland persevered and is known today as the father of the submarine.

Born in County Clare, Ireland, he was educated and trained as a teacher, a profession he practiced for 14 years (1858-72) in various sites throughout Ireland. All during that time, he harbored a dream from his youth: to build a boat that could travel underwater, a boat that could be used against the British Navy in Ireland's fight for independence.

Not that there was any proof or history that such a vehicle could ever be practically employed: in fact, every pervious effort had met with resounding failure.

But those failures never doused the flame of Holland's belief that such a boat could be built and be practical. Unfortunately, he lacked the financial resources needed to make his belief a reality.

In 1873, he moved to the United States, settling in Paterson, NJ, where he was hired as an elementary school teacher at St. John's Parochial School. Soon afterwards, he began shopping his submarine ideas and designs around to the United States Navy, which promptly rejected them as preposterous.

He received financial support from the Irish Republican Brotherhood and built a 14', one-person model, which was tested with success in 1878. Encouraged by that success, the group further financed Holland, who then built a 31', three-person version of the submarine with a one-cylinder internal-combustion engine. It had a depth of 60 feet and embraced many of the principles of submarine design that are still in practice today.

Impatient to build similar vehicles quickly, the Brotherhood then took the project out of the inventor's hands and built a submarine that failed. Undeterred, Holland continued to make designs and improvements on paper. Finally, in 1895, he received a contract from the U.S. Navy to construct a submarine for $150,000. Unfortunately, it wasn't long before a Navy admiral wrested control of the project from Holland and again, it was a failure.

Holland tried again, this time using all of his ideas that had been cast aside by others. The result was the Holland, a 53', 10" submarine with a torpedo tube, a dynamite gun and several Whitehead torpedoes. It is, for all intents and purposes, the first practical submarine ever built--especially since it had the ability to move and maneuver underwater, fueled by its electric batteries. It was also the first submarine able to dive by inclining its axis.

Later in life, Holland invented a respirator to allow crew members to escape from disabled submarines, but it was his invention of the first practical submarine that changed the way wars were fought forever--and earned him a place in history as the father of the submarine.

42

John J. Hughes
Catholic Archbishop; Outspoken Leader

A rchbishop John J. Hughes spent his adult life serving God and the Catholic Church. Through that service, he left legacies to his church and to the public at large, in terms of a new outlook on the role of religion in public education in the United States.

As administrator of the diocese of New York, Hughes entered the controversy over religion and schools in 1840. At that time, the Public School Society, a private organization, controlled most public funding for city schools. The society also provided religious training in those schools, training considered offensive by city Catholics. They sought changes that would provide them a share of public funds for their own schools.

They did not win that funding. But their efforts led to the destruction of the Public School Society, the removal of religion from American public education at all levels and the creation of the parochial school system in the country.

Hughes' path to church leadership began in Ireland. At age 20, he followed his father and an older brother to the United States. He then attempted to follow his long-time interest in the priesthood by entering the seminary. After three years and the intercession of a sympathetic priest, he finally obtained a place as a student at Mt. St. Mary's Seminary in Emmitsburg, Md. He was ordained in 1826 in St. Joseph's Church in Philadelphia.

Hughes was successful as a pastor, but better-known for his writings and sermons. Until his arrival in the Philadelphia area, many Catholics there felt silence was the best response to the rampant anti-Catholicism. Hughes did not agree, and fought instead through pamphlets, letters and a Catholic newspaper.

His leadership and his administrative talents led church leaders to promote the young cleric. In 1838, he became coadjutor of the diocese of New York, making him the designated successor to the bishop. By 1839, however, he was named administrator after the bishop suffered a stroke. He would become bishop in 1842 and archbishop in 1850.

The diocese he led then covered all of New York and about one-half of New Jersey. At the time he became administrator, it included 200,000 Catholics, served by just 22 churches and seven schools. One of his first actions as administrator was a trip to Europe, seeking aid to make needed changes throughout the sprawling diocese.

Over his time in the diocese, he encouraged communities of priests and nuns to locate facilities in the diocese, began construction of the new St. Patrick's Cathedral and founded a seminary and the college at Fordham, which was later transferred to the Jesuit order.

As diocesan leader, Hughes continued to speak his mind. His national reputation grew as New York Catholics, under his leadership, prevented the kind of anti-Catholic riots seen elsewhere in the 1840s. He believed good Catholics could also be good Americans, and encouraged them to support both the pope and the U.S. Constitution.

At the request of President Lincoln, he visited Europe in 1862 to seek support for the Union. Lincoln's government later encouraged the Vatican to name Hughes as the first American cardinal. Their efforts were not successful.

Hughes continued his public role through 1863, when he offered his aid to efforts to stop draft riots in the city of New York.

Many of Hughes' legacies, such as Fordham University, were visible. No less real are the unseen legacies -- for Catholics, a stronger sense of unity with their nation and, perhaps, for some anti-Catholics, a change of mind.

43

Andrew Jackson
U.S. President

He slowly embarked on a democratic journey, starting as a lawyer, and eventually reaching the highest point in American government when he took the title President of the United States.

In 1765, his parents emigrated from Carrickfergus, Ireland. When he was 14, Andrew Jackson became the lone survivor among his parents and siblings. Thirty-seven years later, he was inaugurated as the seventh president.

Jackson began as a lawyer, assisting in state matters. He also served as a delegate in the convention which framed Tennessee's constitution. Jackson won the single seat in the House of Representatives allotted to the new state.

After resigning from the House to focus on other interests, Jackson was elected one of the superior judges of Tennessee. But he wanted more. Jackson longed for the major generalship of the Tennessee militia. Next to the governorship, it was the second-most esteemed position.

A tie stood in the way of obtaining this position, until the tie-breaking vote was cast his way. After spending two years as major general, he retired in 1804, spending the next eight years as a country gentleman.

He was continuing to embark on the democratic journey, experiencing life.

On that journey, the War of 1812 broke out. Jackson was appointed to command portions of the Tennessee forces. Some of his victories resulted in him being commissioned as a major-general in the United States Army, which led to commanding larger battles such as the one at New Orleans. Although the peace treaty to end the war had been signed before the battle to save New Orleans finished, Jackson emerged as a powerful and significant figure in America.

In 1821, President James Monroe appointed Jackson governor of the new territory called Florida. Jackson was setting himself up politically as the 1824 election drew near. He had a desire to lead this country as far as he could.

He lost the 1824 election, and claimed corruption on the part of his opponents. That made his fire grow as he longed to win the presidency. He campaigned personally as a war hero who was wronged. That's all. He did not have any solid programs to announce such as today's politicians. He raised the consciousness of Americans about politics - and won the 1828 election.

Jackson continued his democratic journey, only this time leading the pack.

New men were placed in executive positions as a result of Jackson's victory. The process and system were being cleaned.

In 1832, Jackson ran for re-election. The nominating convention system grew to take its place. Jackson ran on the issue of the day, which was re-chartering the Bank of the United States. People perceived Jackson's anti-bank stance as democracy-in-action and wanted to see results. He was propelled back into the White House for another four years.

Jackson's legacy remains with the Democratic party today. The presidency also grew stronger because of Jackson. Never one to pontificate on issues, he was a realist who faced matters one by one. He understood what was right for Americans as issues arised, such as banking.

Andrew Jackson paved the road even more for future patriots to embark on their journeys through history.

44

Andrew Johnson
U.S. President

The seventeenth president of the United States was born in 1808 to Jacob and Mary (McDunough) Johnson. Jacob died in 1811 when Andrew was three years old, leaving the family poor. Mary's remarriage failed to improve the family's standing and Johnson grew up without any formal education. As young man Johnson apprenticed for a tailor in Raleigh, North Carolina.

Johnson left North Carolina with his mother and step-father in 1826 and settled in Tennessee. After wandering the state for awhile, Johnson took up residence in Greeneville and married a school teacher, Eliza McCardle in 1827. The couple had five children, Martha, Charles, Mary, Robert and Andrew. Eliza also educated her husband while he ran a tailor shop in Greeneville. Johnson, though never a formal student, was able to take part in debates for Greeneville College and Tusculum-Academy. These debates vastly improved his oratory skills.

While he compiled modest wealth as tailor, he embarked on a political career when he was elected an alderman of Greeneville. After consecutive terms as an alderman he was elected mayor and eventually ascended to the state legislature of Tennessee in 1835. Johnson was defeated in 1837 but re-elected in 1839 and in 1841 he won a seat in the state senate.

By 1843 he was making waves in the federal government, as he was elected to the House of Representatives. Johnson served in the House for ten years, then he returned to Tennessee and ran for governor. He was elected and in 1855 served another term. In 1857 he took a seat in the United States Senate. While in the senate he worked on a joint committee on the conduct of war.

In 1862, while still serving in the senate, President Lincoln appointed Johnson military governor of Tennessee, with the special task of establishing the authority of the federal government in the state. After the civil war, in which tore Tennessee in half, Johnson was able to restore civil government, making the state a model for restoration.

Johnson became a nominee for vice president for Lincoln's second run at the office. The stressful campaign coupled with the war left Johnson fatigued and sick, but as the Lincoln-Johnson ticket was successful at the polls, Johnson was summoned to Washington D.C. for the inaugural ceremonies.

In April of 1865 President Lincoln was assassinated and vice-president Johnson ascended to the presidency in a quiet, simple ceremony. As the nation mourned, Johnson announced he would keep Lincoln's cabinet in place and continue with the plans Lincoln had laid.

In the time that followed, Johnson went to battle with Congress over the reconstruction legislation and battled the states that had succeeded over all slavery and readmitedness to the union. Continuous disputes between the president and Congress, coupled with uprisings in the south lead to negative public opinion for the president. Then Johnson lost three members of Lincoln's cabinet, all of which resigned, and he embarked on a speaking tour in the North to raise public favor. However, the tour failed when Johnson was drawn in debate with audiences that had come to hear him speak.

His struggle with Congress continued as the overturned veto after veto on reconstruction legislation. The Republicans began to charge the president with intemperance.

In 1968 Johnson was impeached of high crimes and misdemeanors in office. In the time the trial that followed Johnson narrowly escaped conviction, but at it's end there was less than a year remaining in his term and he sat more or less as a "lamed duck." Johnson ratified the 14th Amendment to the constitution in the waning months of his presidency.

Upon returning to Tennessee, Johnson was drawn into state politics. In 1869 Johnson ran for the Senate but was defeated. He win the race for representative-at-large from Tennessee in 1872. In 1874, though weakened by an attack of yellow fever he was elected to the United States Senate. Johnson regained public favor in that post as his honest dealing stuck out in contrast to the mostly corrupt actions of President Grant's republican administration.

Johnson's reversal of fortune was short lived as he died while still in office on July 31, 1875.

45

James A Joyce
Author

T he author of the greatest novel in the English language nearly became a doctor.

Literature and the 20th century may have turned out quite different had Dublin-born James Joyce followed through on his goal of attending medical school and writing at the same time.

However, he failed to accomplish this both in Dublin and Paris so he focused solely on writing. The world is richer for Joyce's failure.

"Ulysses," his 1922 tail of the day in the life of Dublin natives Stephen Dedalus and Leopold and Molly Bloom, was voted the greatest novel published in English in the summer of 1998. While the list elicited great debate, there was little dissension with number 1.

The surreal, avant-garde novel's influence was not limited to the literary world. The book's publishing was banned in the United States, because some groups considered the book obscene. A 1933 U.S. Supreme Court ruling allowed the book to be published in the U.S. and set the precedent for obscenity cases for decades.

"Ulysses" is simply a masterpiece. On the surface it is a realistic portrayal of city life among the undesirables of Dublin. However, it is also a brilliant exploration of human behavior. Many elements of the book, including the protagonists' last name, invoke the "Odyssey," which has added to the novel's universal appeal.

However, Joyce was no one-hit wonder. his first no el, "A Portrait of the Artist as a Young Man" was well received and was published in The Egoist, one of the most popular magazines of the day. "The Dubliners," a collection of short stories which took Joyce nine year's to get published, were praised for their realism. Like "Ulysses," these stories were also intense examinations of the human condition that continue to influence writers of today.

While Joyce is celebrated as a novelist - deservedly so -, it's often forgotten that Joyce was a poet and a playwright. he published two collections of his poetry and one play, "The Exiles," which was heavily influenced by one of his idols, Norwegian playwright Henrik Ibsen. While neither was a huge success, they stand as testament to his wide-ranging ability as a writer.

The son of a petty politician and office holder, Joyce graduated from Belevedere College in Dublin. While in college, Joyce's early writings were praised by playwright Henrik Ibsen and he visited William Butler Yates before going to Paris.

Despite failing eyesight, which required 10 serious operations on his eyes, Joyce managed to publish a collection of poems, "Pomes Pennyeach" in 1927 and one novel, "Finnegan's Wake" in 1939 following his masterpiece. He was working on a sequel, "The Reawakening," when World War II forced him and his family to move to Switzerland, where he died of a perforated ulcer in early 1941.

In his 59 years, Joyce published only seven works. However, they nearly all rank among the most influential works, and his best, "Ulysses" is also literature's best.

46

Buster Keaton
Famed Comic Actor

One might say that Joseph "Buster" Keaton fell into show business.

Keaton was born in 1895 to Joseph and Myra Keaton, who were stars in vaudeville. He picked up his unusual nickname-and the name the world knew him by-when, at the age of six months, he toppled down a flight of stairs, landing at the bottom unharmed and without a whimper. There, he was picked up by family friend Harry Houdini, who commented after seeing the child's unfazed countenance, that the baby could really endure a fall-or, as he called it, a "buster." The beginning of a nickname-and a legend--was born.

Keaton quickly became part of the family's vaudeville act, and his uncanny ability to fall and take good-natured pummeling, apparently without getting hurt was quickly discovered and used. The Keatons' act was recognized by many as the most rough-and-tumble act in vaudeville, and Buster was the star.

Unfortunately, his father's drinking problems finally broke up the act in 1917, and Keaton moved to Hollywood, where silent movies were the rage, to rekindle his career. There, he happened to meet another comedic legend, Fatty Arbuckle, who took Keaton under his wing and introduced him into the world of silent films, where Keaton's ability to deadpan his way through spills, falls, tumbles and drops were just the perfect ingredients for the comedic recipe of the time.

He went on to make scores of short films and 14 major silent features, stamping himself as one of the greatest of all silent film stars. The New York Times took special note of his unique place in the world of silent film stars, observing, "In a film world that exaggerated everything, and in which every emotion was dramatized and elaborated, he remained impassive and solemn, his poker-faced inscrutability suppressing all emotion."

Keaton later needed that "poker-faced inscrutability" as his stock plummeted in the 1930s. No long the raging star of the silent screen, Keaton was relegated to writing gags for such acts as the Marx Brothers as his movie career in the "talkies" floundered.

His career enjoyed a resurgence in the 1950s when he appeared in Charlie Chaplin's film, "Limelight." That sparked renewed interest in his earlier work, and also gave him scores of guest shots on the nation's newest emerging medium, television. He enjoyed some success with his own television show, "The Buster Keaton Comedy Show," and appeared on TV with many stars of the new medium, including Ed Sullivan and Gary Moore.

After two failed marriages, he finally found success with his third wife, Eleanor Norris, who was more than 20 years his junior. His friends cautioned against the marriage, sensing it was ill-fated, but the couple proved them wrong and Keaton finally found marital happiness.

He died in 1966, shortly after finishing work on his last movie, "A Funny Thing Happened on the Way to the Forum." He left behind a legacy of comedic genius that is still appreciated today.

47

Michael Keaton
Actor

Reprising the role of a popular superhero always meets criticism from movie fans and reviewers alike. When director Tim Burton cast Michael Keaton in the title role of the movie "Batman," many questioned the comedic actor's range and ability to play the part. When the movie opened to rave reviews internationally, groans were quieted, critics approved and sequels were developed.

Keaton storied career in show business began after the actor dropped out of Kent State University and was cast in a PBS documentary on mental illness. Keaton, who played a deranged man, took the experience as a calling. "I realized I'd better try to be a comedian." Born Michael Douglas, the Pennsylvania native would go on to perform standup comedy and work in various comedy troupes.

The silver screen called Keaton in 1982, when director Ron Howard paired him with Henry Winkler in the movie Night Shift, about two workers in a New York City morgue who ran a prostitution ring in their offices. The movie opened to stunning reviews for his film debut. Chicago Tribune movie critic Gene Siskel in a 1982 review commented, "Based on this one role, I would pay to see Keaton in anything." The public came calling again in 1983 when he played one of his landmark roles-a laid off car designer who switched roles in the house with his wife-in Mr. Mom. A string of slapstick comedies would follow, including the star-studded Johnny Dangerously (1984) and Gung Ho (1986). Each would be both critical and financial failures.

Keaton's rebounded with the first of four memorable movies. Beetlejuice (1988) saw the return of funnyman Keaton, who's character was resurrected by two deceased homeowners (played by Jeff Daniels and Geena Davis) to rid their house of the new, obnoxious owners. One of the most successful and funny movies of the year, it set the stage for one of his most profound roles. Clean and Sober found Keaton as a cocaine and alcohol addict who realizes he has a problem. As his friends overdose and die around him, Keaton's character goes through the drama of curing himself. His touching performance earned him the National Society of Film Critics "Best Actor" award.

Cast as Batman (1989), Keaton found critical success with the movie in a role he almost turned down. In an interview with Rolling Stone's Bill Zehme (June 29, 1989), Keaton admitted that he read the part as a courtesy before finding the role to his liking. "When Tim (Burton) first came to me with the script, I read it out of politeness. All the while, I'm thinking there's no way I'd do this." Batman grossed $475 million worldwide, vaulting him into the upper echelon of movie actors and earned him a repeat performance as the "Caped Crusader" in the 1992 followup Batman Returns (1992).

In a world where actors are a dime a dozen, it was an Irish actor who gave two of the most memorable performances-in Mr. Mom and in the Batman series-of this generation.

48

Emmett Kelly

Circus Clown

Emmett Kelly is best known for his creation of Weary Willie, the forlorn little hobo who starred for many years in the Ringling Brothers, Barnum and Bailey Circus. But neither creator nor creation was originally headed for the spotlights of the circus.

Instead, Weary Willie was first created during an earlier Kelly career, as a cartoonist with the Adagram Film Company of Kansas City. When Willie first showed up, his creator believed, as he had since childhood, that he would earn his living as an artist.

Kelly had shown artistic ability from childhood, but had little formal training. He attended school only through the eighth grade, spending his time after that working with his family on their farm. His mother, noting her son's talent, did invest in a correspondence course in cartooning. It proved to be an inspired choice.

Kelly's first job as a cartoonist held a prediction of what he would do later in life. He began giving chalk talks, using his cartooning skills to illustrate the points he was making. He would continue those talks through his life, using them often during nightclub performances.

Shortly after obtaining the Adagram job, Kelly attended a circus. His next career direction was in sight, as he handled several jobs with the circus and fell in love with "trouping," living on the road and performing.

His first real circus job began in 1921, when he signed a contract with Howe's Great London Circus. He then was considered primarily a trapeze artist who could double as a clown as needed. Problems with his trapeze act left him performing solely as a clown during that contract, although he returned to the trapeze the following year with John Robinson's Circus.

By 1931, however, it was clear Kelly would be a clown. After searching unsuccessfully for a trapeze job, he accepted a clown position in 1931 with the Hagenbeck-Wallace Circus. While working there, he decided "if I were going to have to spend all my time in Clown Alley, I would not be just another clown, but would try to create something special."

Weary Willie came to life. In later years, Kelly would explain that clowning is something that has to be "inside you, a way of feeling about things that comes out somehow if you get the opportunity." Kelly never felt, however, that he could explain why audiences found Willie funny.

Another Kelly description of Willie may explain why audiences welcomed him. He said the little hobo "always got the short end of the stick and never had any good luck at all, but .. never lost hope and just kept trying."

Through his years with the circus, Kelly married three times, each time to a fellow circus performer. Two of those marriages ended in divorce.

By 1956, Kelly decided to retire from the circus, in part to spend more time with the younger two of his four children. He had not, however, retired Weary Willie. Instead, Willie appeared everywhere from nightclubs to the Brooklyn Dodgers' baseball games. He had appeared in the movies and Broadway before his retirement and assisted with a television program on his life afterward.

Kelly's clowning earned him a place, after his death, in the Clown Hall of Fame. He had decided long before that he was pleased with the places Willie had taken him.

"I couldn't say that life with the circus is the softest deal in the world," Kelly said, "but I would rather live out my life in Clown Alley than in a marble palace."

49

Gene Kelly
Legendary Star of Musicals

hat the world of sports lost, the world of movie musicals gained.

Gene Kelly never lived his dream of becoming a professional baseball player, but he went on to become one of the most famous stars of movie and broadway's musicals of all time, using his vaunted athletic skills on the stage rather than on the field.

His classic film, "Singing in the Rain," is considered a masterpiece and one of the best-loved musicals of all-time. Included in that movie is Kelly's epic performance of the film's title song, when he splashes and dances his way through a four-minute routine that emblazons a lasting memory on viewers' minds for its genius and Kelly's sheer ease of movement.

Eugene Kelly was born on August 23, 1912, the middle of five children and the offspring of James and Harriet Curran Kelly. His father was a phonograph salesman, and his mother involved herself in making certain her children had an appreciation for the arts. So talented were the children that the quintet-known as the Five Kellys-was an oft-seen local amateur vaudeville act in the native Pittsburgh.
oft-seen local amateur vaudeville act in the native Pittsburgh.

Much to his chagrin, Kelly was forced, along with his brother, to take dance lessons, which he dreaded. But as he grew older and discovered girls, he also discovered that his innate and honed ability to dance made him popular with them…and suddenly, dancing wasn't so bad.

97

He enjoyed stints in his young life as a vaudeville act with his brother (The Kelly Brothers) and founded the Gene Kelly Studio of Dance in Pittsburgh, where he discovered he enjoyed teaching dance. A 1933 graduate of the University of Pittsburgh, Kelly earned a degree in economics and actually began pursuing a degree in law. But the lure of the stage was stronger than the lure of law, and Kelly left Pittsburgh and traveled to Broadway in 1938 to see how far his feet could take him.

Of course, those dancing feet took him to stardom, beginning with his breakthrough performance as Harry the Hoofer in the Broadway play, "The Time of Your Life." Another break came in 1940 on Broadway, when he played Joey Evans in "Pal Joey," a play that ran for 270 performances. His stellar performance in that play attracted the interest of Hollywood, and in 1941, Kelly left the lights of Broadway for the lure of Hollywood. It was a brilliant career choice.

He debuted in movies in "For Me and My Gal," which starred Judy Garland, and followed that with a series of smaller roles and choreograph chores in lesser known movies, breaking through again when he starred with Rita Hayworth in "Cover Girl." Then came "Anchors Aweigh," which earned him an Academy Award nomination for best actor.

He did win an Oscar in 1951 for his "extreme versatility as an actor, singer, director and dancer, but specifically for his brilliant achievement in the art of choreography on film" for his part in the class "An American in Paris," which copped the best picture Oscar that year.

His career began to wane in the late 1950s, and his personal life also suffered, as he ended his 15-year marriage to his first wife, Betsy, and he became disenchanted with his long-time studio, MGM. He remarried in 1960 to Jeanne Coyne, his dance assistant, and they had two children. Unfortunately, in 1973, Jeanne died from cancer. In 1990, he remarried Patricia Ward.

Gene Kelly died on February 2, 1996, but his legend lives on. The person who wanted to be a major league baseball player for the Pittsburgh Pirates instead went down in history as one of the world's greatest entertainers, a legendary actor whose dancing made his performances immortal.

50

Grace Kelly

Legendary Actress, Princess

H er life is a mix of a fairy tale and a Shakespearean tragedy, complete with heady success, fabled romance and a tragic, all-too-early ending. Her tale is one of turning her back on movie stardom for the man she loved, of leaving her native country for his, and of devoting her life to her family rather than to her career.

Born Grace Patricia Kelly on November 12, 1929, in Philadelphia, Pennsylvania, to John and Margaret Kelly, she enjoyed a comfortable childhood, thanks to the business of her father, who was a well-to-do contractor.

From early on, it appears that Grace was fascinated with acting and had decided at an early age to pursue her dreams at the earliest opportunity. That opportunity came in 1947, following her graduation from high school, when she moved to New York to test her talent there.

Though she had some success as a model and on Broadway, Grace decided that what she really wanted to do was to act in films and, to do that, she had to move to southern California. She achieved that goal at the relatively young age of 22, acting in her first movie, "Fourteen Hours," in 1951. She went on to appear in High Noon in 1952 and in Mogambo in 1953. She had become a star-a role that she cemented with her performance in the great Alfred Hitchcock's movie, "Rear Window." She worked again with Hitchcock in "Dial M for Murder."

Her crowning moment in film came, however, in 1954, when she won the Best Actress Award for her portrayal of Georgie Elgin in the movie, "The Country Girl," playing opposite the legendary Bing Crosby. As an additional accomplishment, her rendition of the song "True Love" from a subsequent movie ("High Society") won her a gold record.

It was while working in the French Riviera on another Hitchcock movie, "To Catch a Thief," that she became enchanted with some beautiful gardens she saw while riding along the countryside. They turned out to be the garden's of Prince Rainier Grimaldi III of Monaco, whom she would later meet at the Cannes Film Festival.

She fell in love with Grimaldi and married him in 1956. In her role as princess, she was obligated to forsake her acting career, a career that had spawned 11 films and millions of fans across the world.

She gave to the Prince the heirs he always wanted, giving birth to three children-Caroline, Albert and Stephanie. Without an heir, and upon the death of the Prince, Monaco would have reverted to become once again part of France, and its citizens would pay French taxes.

Tragically, she died on September 14, 1982, when the car she was in went off a road on the cliffs of her adopted country, Monaco. She was less than a month shy of her 53rd birthday when the accident occurred.

She left behind a double legacy-one of acting greatness and one of royalty-and endures today as a princess in both the world of film and in Monaco.

51

John F. Kennedy
U.S. President

A personal reflection by the author:

I can honestly say that no individual in this book-no matter how heroic they were in their lives-has touched me as deeply and as movingly as did the life of John F. Kennedy. In a very real way, I feel I had a personal relationship with him, because of some parallel events in his life and in the life of my family.

In 1960, when he was running for the presidency on the United States, my father, John L. Bartimole, was running for Mayor of Derby, Connecticut, the state's smallest city. The parallels between my father's political life and JFK's were evident: both had become upset winners in their primaries to become their party's Democratic standard-bearers, and both were beloved in their home areas.

On a cold October night, I was awakened by my parents from a sound sleep and told "it's time to meet the next president of the United States." Because my father headed the Democratic ticket in Derby, he was being given the honor of greeting JFK has he rode through the city in a motorcade.

When we arrived on Main Street in downtown Derby, Connecticut, I couldn't believe my eyes: thousands of people lined both sides of the road, hoping to get glimpse of this young, vibrant candidate for the presidency. The early autumn chill didn't deter or diminish the crowd, nor did the fact that the motorcade arrived hours after it was supposed to.

101

The crowd erupted when the motorcade came into view, and the air was electric as Kennedy's car paused beneath the traffic light at the corners of Elizabeth Street and Main. Though I was just six years old, the scene is forever emblazoned in my mind: an incredibly handsome, energetic young man, oozing with personality and charm, smiling broadly at thousands of people who waved frantically to him. I can still see the boyish face, the gleaming hair, the twinkled eyes, as my father approached him, extended his hand, and welcomed him to Derby.

The whole event couldn't have lasted for more than a few minutes, but I can replay it forever in my mind. Something clicked that night between my father and JFK, too. When he became president, JFK visited Gracie Mansion in New York City to meet with Mayor Robert F. Wagner, and my father was one of a select group of mayors to be invited. Sadly, my father was also invited to JFK's funeral after his tragic assassination.

Volumes have been written about JFK's heroics and his indiscretions, but perception remains reality to me, and I prefer to remember Kennedy as the shining star who rode into my hometown early one morning and transformed-if only for a moment-the tiny city of Derby, Connecticut, into Camelot.

52

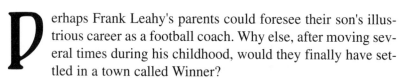

Frank Leahy
Football Coach

Perhaps Frank Leahy's parents could foresee their son's illustrious career as a football coach. Why else, after moving several times during his childhood, would they finally have settled in a town called Winner?

Leahy proved he could be a football winner in his first head coaching job, a two-year stint at Boston College. Before Leahy, B.C. was the "easy win" on other teams' schedules. In his first year as coach, however, he re-energized the team and led them to a nearly-undefeated season.

The following year, he corrected that one "mistake;" his team went 10-0 in the regular season. They capped that success by an underdog win in the Sugar Bowl, a 19-13 defeat of Tennessee.

But Leahy's roots were calling. His alma mater, Notre Dame, offered him their head coaching job. Although he had just signed a contract extension with B.C., he asked for his release and accepted the Notre Dame job.

Leahy's football career began at Notre Dame 14 years earlier, as a member of one of Knute Rockne's Irish teams. He was not the most talented member of the Notre Dame team, but his determination and hard work made him a successful offensive lineman. He was the starting right tackle on Notre Dame's national championship team of 1929.

103

A knee injury in 1930 forced Leahy to refocus his energies. As it became obvious he would not play again, he talked football, often, with Rockne, absorbing new football lessons. Rockne then reinforced those lessons by naming Leahy as coach for the tackles. That experience led him to a career as a coach, starting in 1931 as an assistant at Georgetown.

From Georgetown, Leahy took assistant jobs at Michigan State and Fordham. He was the coach who developed Fordham's "Seven Blocks of Granite," including a lineman named Vince Lombardi, who would also attain fame in the NFL as the Green Bay Packers coach.

As Notre Dame's coach, Leahy continued his winning ways, leading the Irish through their first undefeated season in 11 years. Through time, he added new (and now accepted) football moves, including the "pocket" to protect the quarterback. He also found time to write two books on football.

After two years of Navy service, Leahy returned to Notre Dame. His teams remained undefeated for four seasons before finally losing a game to Purdue in 1950. Three years later, his team again went undefeated, but a combination of factors, including poor health, led to a resignation at the end of that season.

Leahy's later business career was not as successful as his coaching. However, he remained quite popular on the lecture circuit throughout the last 20 years of his life.

As a head coach, Leahy led teams to seven undefeated seasons and four national championships. His teams also produced four players who won Heisman trophies. His parents may not have been able to see the future, but their choice of a town named Winner definitely foreshadowed their son's coaching career.

53

James Logan
Colonial Statesman, Judge

H is contributions to Pennsylvania history are substantial, but it's not unusual for people to never have heard of James Logan, because he spent much of his career bolstering and enhancing the efforts of his good friend, William Penn, as they built the colony during pre-Revolutionary days.

If he had his way as a young boy, Logan--who, thanks to his father's diligence, was well-versed in Greek, Latin and Hebrew by the age of 13--might have had a remarkably different course in life. In 1697, at the age of 23, he wished to travel to Jamaica, but his mother objected and he abided by his mother's wishes. Instead, he began dabbling in the shipping trade between Dublin, his birthplace, and Bristol, England, where his family had settled.

During those transactions, he met William Penn and impressed him immediately with his knowledge and talents. Penn invited him to sail with him to Pennsylvania in 1699, and a long-lasting friendship was born.

Logan spent 52 years in service to Pennsylvania, rising from Penn's secretary to various lofty ranks, including State Supreme Court Justice and mayor of the city of Philadelphia. He was the chief executive of the Province of Pennsylvania (1736-38) during its brief border war with Maryland and had previously served as Philadelphia's mayor in 1722.

He was a rarity among scholars because he believed that defensive fighting was justifiable, an opinion not shared by his friend, Penn, a confirmed pacifist. Logan carried those views throughout his life, and often argued that those who opposed funding armies and other means of defense should not seek election to public office.

His judicial career began in 1726 when the governor of the province appointed him as a justice of Philadelphia County. His career on the bench progressed rapidly from there, with stops as judge of the court of common pleas, to the State Supreme Court, and finally, in 1731, as chief justice of the State Supreme Court.

Logan was particularly interested in how gentlemen of society should comport themselves, which he addressed in his "Charges Delivered from the Bench to the Grand Inquest...1736."

He married Sarah Reed, daughter of a prominent merchant, and had five children with her. A reader with a voracious appetite, Logan left his considerable library of 3,000 books to the city of Philadelphia upon his death.

So, while Logan's place in Pennsylvania's history may have been behind the scenes and one of support, his impact on the province and , eventually, the country were great: not only did his political beliefs and his philosophy on fighting seem to anticipate the Revolutionary War, his time on the State Supreme Court helped set the tone for justice in the area for years to come.

54

Connie (McGillicuddy) Mack

Baseball Manager

Perhaps Connie Mack, one of baseball's greatest managers, had the perfect perspective on what managing was all about. "Managing," Mack was fond of saying, "is twelve and a half percent strategy; twelve and a half percent is comprised of what a manager can get out of his team. The other 75 percent is talent."

When Mack had talent, his managing prowess was extraordinary, but what was always astounding was his ability to spot talent and to wring every ounce of talent from his teams.

He managed an astounding 7,878 games in a career that stretched from 1894 until 1950, when he voluntarily replaced himself at the age of 88. His record is Hall of Fame material: he won 3,776 games, but lost 4,025, and his team finished last 17 times. He lead his teams to nine pennants and five World Series championships.

But Mack, the distinguished manager of the Philadelphia Athletics from 1901 to his retirement in 1950, was a baseball original, a man whose contributions to baseball cannot be measured by wins and losses, but by his indelible impact on the game of baseball.

Born in East Brookfield, Mass., on Feb. 22, 1862, Cornelius Alexander McGillicuddy was one of nine children. His formal education ended in sixth grade, when he quit school to work in a cotton mill. Certainly he loved the fledgling game of baseball--also known as four o'cat or roundball--more than he loved formal education or working in the cotton mill.

107

So, when he was offered a job in March of 1994 as the catcher for the Meriden (Conn.) baseball team, he jumped at the $80/month opportunity. His name was shortened to Mack by a reporter who complained, "McGillicuddy will never fit in to the boxscore!"

Various stops along the way in places such as Washington, Pittsburgh and Buffalo typified his professional baseball playing career, which was severely hampered by a fractured ankle he suffered in 1893 in a game against Boston. In his playing career, he appeared in 723 games in a 10-year span, hit .,245 with 5 home runs and 265 RBIs--certainly not Hall of Fame material.

But Mack was then given the opportunity to manage near the end of his playing career in 1894, when he was appointed the manager of the Pittsburgh franchise of the National League for the season's final 23 games. He remained as a player-manager until 1896, but then was fired. After a stint as a manager of the Milwaukee franchise of the Western League, he became manager of the Philadelphia franchise of the upstart newcomer in major league baseball, the American League.

There he stayed until 1950, a remarkable half-century run with the same team. During that career, he managed such greats as Mickey Cochrane, Jimmie Foxx, Eddie Blank, Bobby Shantz, George Kell, Jack Coombs, Lefty Grove and Chief Bender.

The staunch Catholic who had endured so long in baseball, however, never considered baseball his entire life. He once said, "If I had to write my own epitaph, it would read: He loved his God, his home, his country, his fellow men, and baseball."

55

Charles William Mayo

Surgeon

Medicine was not a surprising career choice for Charles W. Mayo. His father and uncle were doctors and his mother, Edith, was a nurse. His grandfather, also a doctor, founded the well-known Mayo Clinic after a tornado struck his Minnesota home.

The younger Mayo started his own medical career with training at the University of Pennsylvania and the Robert Packer Hospital in Sayre, Pennsylvania. He then returned to Minnesota for a four-year fellowship in surgery, the specialty of both his father and uncle. Once home, Mayo would continue working at the family clinic through the rest of his life.

Mayo served as a member of the clinic's board of governors from 31 years, from 1933 to 1964. He also served on the board of regents for the University of Minnesota, helping to direct the activities of the Mayo Foundation for Medical Education and Research.

The doctor left his post, but not his clinic affiliation, during World War II, when he saw active duty in the Army Medical Corps. He served at a number of clinic-affiliated hospitals, including a period as commanding officer of a hospital in New Guinea.

After the war, Mayo continued to blend medical work with public service. He developed a specialty in diseases of the colon. He served on the national medical advisory board of the American Legion, offering testimony before Congress on government medical facilities.

Another challenge also awaited Mayo. From the creation of the United Nations, the United States appointed a professional to its delegation each year. In 1953, Mayo was selected as that professional. He had not expected the appointment, but it became, in his words, "a wonderful sabbatical from the clinic."

During his service at the United Nations, Mayo drew on his scientific background to help answer accusations that the United States had used germ warfare in Korea. "Confessions" of such practices, he told a committee of the General Assembly, were coerced from American soldiers by torture.

Later, he encouraged Americans to continue to support the United Nations. The organization, he said, "can be no stronger than the expressed interest and intelligent public opinion of the peoples of those sixty nations who are members of the United Nations."

Although his tenure on the United Nations delegation lasted only one year, Mayo's commitment to public service and to medicine continued throughout his life.

56

John McCormack

Statesman, Government Leader

H is humble--indeed, poverty-stricken--beginnings gave no hint of the fame and fortune that were to be his decades down the road. But John McCormack, the first Roman Catholic ever to serve as Speaker of the House of Representatives, managed to overcome a childhood and early adulthood that would have consumed the passions and potential of most to rise to one of the most powerful positions in Federal government.

As Speaker of the House of Representatives, he succeeded the legendary Sam Rayburn, bringing with him a much different style than his predecessor: not only was he as knowledgeable and deft with the facts as was Rayburn, he was also noted for his thoroughness, his attention to minute details, his ability to appease liberals and conservatives alike, and his famous barbed wit. Legend has it he was also a skilled poker player, a trait that was important in building friendships during his early days on the Hill.

McCormack's family was no stranger to ill fortune. All of his grandparents came to the United Sates during the great Irish potato famine if the late 1840s, seeking to build a better life in America. Additionally, of the 12 children born to McCormack's parents, nine died in early childhood

Certainly, it was a rough life for McCormack, made even more difficult just after his elementary school graduation when his father died. Forced to become the family breadwinner, McCormack left school and began selling newspapers to support his family. He left that job to take a position--for the princely sum of $3.50/week--with a local brokerage house, running errands.

What he calls the turning point in his life occurred when he quit that job to accept a position with William T. Way, a lawyer, for $4/week. Way encouraged McCormack to read and to study for the bar examination, and McCormack did so voraciously.

At the age of 21, he passed the bar, which was a bittersweet victory: he beloved mother had died just three months prior to his receiving notification of his personal victory.

As a lawyer, he enjoyed incredible success, beginning his own firm (McCormack and Hardy) and building a reputation as one of the northeast's best trial lawyers.

His political career began in 1917, when he participated in the Massachusetts Constitutional Convention; later, he earned a seat in the State House of Representatives in 1920, and, after an unsuccessful primary bid to unseat incumbent Congressman James A. Gallivan in the state's 12th Congressional District, was elected to that seat upon Gallivan's death.

McCormack immediately stamped himself as a talented, conscientious Congressman, earning a quick appointment to the powerful Ways and Means Committee in just his second term. In 1961, when Speaker Rayburn fell ill, McCormack was appointed Speaker Pro Tempore for the last four weeks of that term and, in January, 1962, following the death of Rayburn, assumed the position on a permanent basis.

McCormack's career still stands today as mute testimony to the ability of one man to rise above difficult beginnings to achieve greatly--in this case, to being the person third in the line to the presidency of the United States.

57

George S. McGovern
U.S. Senator, presidential candidate

Today, most people remember Senator George McGovern as the man whose ill-fated presidential campaign lost badly to incumbent Richard Nixon in the 1972 elections. But that would be to deeply underestimate the value and contributions of a many who devoted much of his life to the service of his country.

Certainly, his performance in the 1972 election was less than stellar. His campaign stumbled almost before it even began, with a divided convention nominating McGovern, whose strong anti-Vietnam War stance angered many of the party faithful. But McGovern's appeal to younger delegates at the convention was enough to give him the nomination.

Trouble arose quickly when the media revealed that his selection for vice president, Senator Thomas Eagleton, had been treated for depression. McGovern hastily replaced Eagleton with R. Sargent Shriver, and the stage was set for political disaster.

That occurred when McGovern carried only the District of Columbia and Massachusetts en route to gaining only 38% of the popular vote. McGovern's career was hurt badly by that performance, causing him to lose in 1980 re-election bid to the Senate and to fail in a quest to again be the party's standard-bearer in 1984.

Still, his contributions to the United States are many and varied. He served from 1957-61 in the U.S. House of Representatives, and as the Director of the Food for Peace program from 1961-62. He was elected to the U.S. Senate in 1962, becoming the first Democrat to be elected to the Senate from South Dakota in 26 years.

Even the fact that he was a Democrat--bucking his family's long-time conservatism and Republican affiliation--demonstrated the free-thinking that characterized McGovern's life. He registered as a Democrat because he felt, from an historical perspective, that the party had better represented the American people. His parents, to their credit, never questioned his party affiliation because, "...they believed that each individual must follow his own conscience in matters of mind and spirit," he later explained.

McGovern earned his Ph.D. from Northwestern University and taught for four years (1949-53) at his undergraduate alma mater, Dakota Wesleyan University before leaving to become the secretary of the South Dakota Democratic party. In 1956, he became the first Democrat elected to the House of Representatives in 22 years, leaving that office to accept a position from President John F. Kennedy as the director of his Food-for-Peace program. He then sought the Senate seat held by Joseph H. Bottum, who had been appointed to fill the unexpired term of Francis Case, who had died while in office.

Perhaps McGovern's most enduring legacy is his love for peace--a love that probably cost him the 1972 election. "The most important issue of our time is the establishment of the condition of world peace," he said. Those words ring as true today as they did more than a quarter-century ago.

58

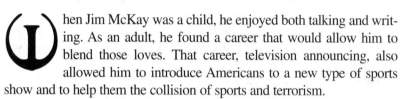

Jim McKay
Sportscaster

hen Jim McKay was a child, he enjoyed both talking and writing. As an adult, he found a career that would allow him to blend those loves. That career, television announcing, also allowed him to introduce Americans to a new type of sports show and to help them the collision of sports and terrorism.

It was that collision of sports and terrorism that truly made McKay's name as a talented broadcaster. McKay was a member of ABC's team at the 1972 Olympics in Munich, when a group of Arabs broke into the Israeli team dormitory, killing two Israelis immediately and holding nine others hostage.

McKay became the voice of that event for Americans. Remaining on location for 15 hours, he kept the ABC audience informed of events, ending with the deaths of all of the hostages. It was McKay who, after the deaths, wondered on the air about the possibility of "any hope and solace for this poor old world."

Through the hours of his broadcast from Munich, McKay "was looking the way we all felt, saying what we were all thinking," said one reporter afterward. "As millions of Americans felt they were helped through the assassination of President Kennedy by the composed commentary of Frank McGee at NBC, McKay played a similar role at Munich."

Before then, the reporter added, McKay had been "a casual acquaintance. Today he's an old pal."

In the years before and after Munich, McKay was primarily introducing American viewers to a new variety of sports, from surfing to log rolling. Skeptics argued no one would care, but ABC's Wide World of Sports proved them wrong. McKay joined the program in 1961; it remains on the air in 1998, still bringing viewers the "thrill of victory and the agony of defeat." Recently, McKay has stepped back from the host duties, but he continues to serve as a sports commentator for ABC.

Hints of the future broadcaster were obvious even in high school and college. McKay played some sports, but was also heavily involved in dramatics, the campus newspaper and debating. After graduation from Loyola University, he spent three years in the United States Navy, then began looking for a job in radio.

Those early efforts were unsuccessful, and McKay ended up with a job of the Baltimore Evening Sun. When the Sun began operating a television station, however, McKay found a place to start his broadcasting career. He shifted to television, filling a variety of announcing duties.

CBS-TV in New York lured McKay away from Baltimore in 1950. His first CBS assignment earned him his stage name. The producer was adamant about calling the show The Real McKay, and the announcer changed his name (originally McManus) to fit the show title.

McKay spent 10 years with CBS, handling a variety of assignments there. One writer said he showed "extraordinary composure before a microphone, a vast fund of diverse information, a quick mind and an ability to talk for however long is necessary without becoming dull or repetitive."

The shift from CBS came in 1960, when he opted not to move to California with his current program. That is when ABC approached him with an unusual offer -- they wanted him to anchor a program about less-known sports. That pairing of announcer and program brought both to fame and 12 Emmys and many other awards to McKay. It has also landed him in both the Sportscasters Hall of Fame and the U.S. Olympic Hall of Fame.

Perhaps the best tribute to McKay's ability comes from the pen of his wife, television columnist Margaret McManus.

"Jim has an infallible eye for the human story behind the sport, so even if you don't much care about the score, you get interested in the people," McManus wrote. "Jim McKay will undoubtedly grow into old age in the classic version of the Irish story-teller, spinning his yarns on the front porch of a summer's night."

59

William McKinley

U.S. President

Twenty-fifth out of 50, seventh out of nine, third of four, first of many - William McKinley was a president, son, assassin victim and leader.

Born in Niles, Ohio, McKinley was known for his serious demeanor and dignity even as a child. After serving in the Ohio Volunteer Regiment - under future President Rutherford B. Hayes - he went to law school and soon passed the bar. A supporter of Hayes' run for Ohio governor, he was elected to Congress in 1871. Throughout his years in Congress, McKinley's pet issue was that of the protective tariff. A contentious issue at the turn of the century, McKinley saw the tariff as a national policy, not a favor for special interests. In helping to pass the McKinley Bill, he saw the passing of the tariff even though it resulted in a landslide defeat for the Republican Party.

After years in Congress, two terms as governor of Ohio and permanent chairman of the Republican Party, McKinley won the Republican nomination for President in 1896. He faced William Jennings Bryan, the most famous politician in U.S. history never elected president. The main issue of this campaign was backing of U.S. currency. McKinley pushed for the gold standard, while Bryan and other westerners fervently favored a silver standard. This was one of the most passionate, contentious presidential campaigns in the nation's history, including Bryan's famous "Cross of Gold" speech. In the end, McKinley won the presidency, becoming the first president to win a popular majority since 1872.

The first half of McKinley's first term was relatively calm. He delayed putting the nation on the gold standard, and along with Congress pursued a "laissez-faire" attitude towards growing industry. In 1898, McKinley made the difficult decision of declaring war on Spain, after that country was accused of blowing up the U.S.S. Maine in Havana harbor. The war was a smashing US success, and the country gained control of land in the Caribbean and the South Pacific. The nation also annexed Hawaii during this time.

In 1900, after being re-elected, he finally tackled the issue of his first campaign. Through the Gold Standard Act, he established gold as the backing of the U.S. currency. This move helped establish the nation as one of the world's economic powers.

Sadly, McKinley was not able to fulfill all his promise as president. While visiting the 1901 Pan-American Exposition in Buffalo, President McKinley became the third U.S. President to be assassinated when he was shot by anarchist Leon Czolgosz on Sept. 6. McKinley died eight days later. Even in death, McKinley had an impact. The creation and proliferation of the Secret Service as presidential bodyguards was a result of McKinley's death, a tribute to one of our forgotten but most influential presidents.

60

Rod McKuen
Poet, Composer, Singer

One of the most prolific, intimate, popular writers and singers in 20th century America, Rod McKuen used the despair and heartbreak of his youth to touch emotional chords in millions of people with his haunting laments about loneliness and unrequited love.

McKuen, an elementary school dropout who was born in an Oakland, Calif., Salvation Army Hospital and whose father deserted him before birth, left school at the tender age of 11, opting to forsake a life that brought him no fulfillment. He wandered from state to state and from job to job, working as a ranch hand, a salesman, and a cookie puncher before settling in the San Francisco area.

By the age of 16, he made his performing debut, landing the lead in the San Francisco Young Players' production of Romeo and Juliet. But it was another break that occurred at roughly the same time that launched McKuen's meteoric career: he became a late-night disc jockey on KROW in Oakland, where he one night mourned on the air about his romantic frustrations and problems.

That lament touched a chord in his young listening audience, as adolescents began to write to him about their problems. A shrewd marketer of his talents even then, McKuen began offering advice to these lovelorn youth in between records.

After spending two years in the Army, McKuen was hired as a singer at the Purple Onion, a San Francisco night club, where he sang folk songs, a genre of music just coming into vogue. Unable to find enough material to perform, McKuen began writing his own folk songs which were a hit with his audiences.

His first legitimate nation-wide hit was "Mr. Oliver Twist," a rock tune that capitalized on the popularity of the Twist, the dance fad that was sweeping the nation in 1961. McKuen performed the song at 80 bowling alleys from coast to coast, and the strain on his voice forced him to stop singing for several months. When he resumed signing, his voice--which had been a tenor--had deepened to a gritty baritone.

While critics cringed over his new voice, McKuen's fans said it gave his performances a new intimacy that injected even more power into his songs.

 McKuen's popularity became entrenched in Glenn Yarbrough recorded an album entitled, "The Lonely Things," which was a collection of McKuen poems set to music. McKuen told an RCA Victor publicist that one of the poems Yarbrough recorded, "Stanyan Street," was from a book he had written, "Stanyan Street and Other Sorrows." Unfortunately, the book didn't exist-- McKuen hadn't written it--but demand for the title was so great the McKuen went on to write and self-publish it, selling more than 65,000 copies before it was acquired by Random House.

While critics debate the relative merits of McKuen's great body of work, his legions of fans make him a popular, if not critical, success. He has sold millions of books and records, composed scores for movies and television shows, and has performed to sold-out audiences across the country.

His real accomplishment, though, is in the way he has touched the hearts of his fans with his rare combination of unique voice, heart-wrenching writing, and his ability to make those who enjoy his musings feel he is talking directly to and about them.

61

Marshall (Herbert) McLuhan

Communications Visionary and Theorist

Marshall McLuhan's impact on communications can't be found in an invention or an improvement of an existing device, but in the revolutionary way he looked at how we communicate--and how messages themselves are at least partially defined by the "box" that they come in.

McLuhan, whose parents were of Scotch-Irish descent, totally revamped the theory of how we communicate with his insightful observation, "The medium is the message." His point was--and is-- simple: that the medium itself, be it television, computers, e-mail, newspapers, magazine, etc., is as much, if not more, of the message as the message itself.

McLuhan originally intended to become an engineer and enrolled at the University of Manitoba in that major. A voracious reader, McLuhan said he "read my way out of engineering and into English literature," earning his bachelor's in that field in 1933, with a master's in 1934.

By 1936, he was teaching at the University of Wisconsin, where his curiosity about the impact of culture and communications on the young was piqued. "I was confronted with young Americans I was incapable of understanding," he said. "I felt an urgent need to study their popular culture in order to get through."

That path led McLuhan to the beginnings of his theories on communications. In his early work on the subject, "The Mechanical Bride: Folklore of Industrial Man," McLuhan lambastes "the pressures set up around us today by the mechanical agencies of the press, radio, moves and advertising."

As his theories evolved, McLuhan's reputation as a communications expert grew. From 1953-55, he chaired a Ford Foundation seminar on culture and communication. In the late 1950s,he was a director of a media project for the United Sates Office of Education and the National Association of Educational Broadcasters.

McLuhan asserted that the advent of movable type was a watershed event in the history of communication, causing the printed word to replace the spoken word as the most important communications medium. Linear forms of print, made economical by movable type, led, theorized McLuhan, to similar linear developments in music, math and the sciences. More importantly, the ear became secondary to the eye as the principal sensory communications organ, a conclusion by McLuhan which forms the basis of his famous "medium is the message" conclusion.

"...a medium is not something neutral--it does something to people," he explained in a one-hour NBC-TV program in 1967. "It rubs them off, it massages them, it bumps them around..."

A practical application of McLuhan's theory would hold that a letter sent in an overnight delivery envelope would be viewed as more important as one delivered by regular mail.

Today, McLuhan's work is even more important, as the impact of several new communications media--from cell phones to e-mail, form faxes to beepers--becomes more pervasive each day. And his work continues to be studied at leading communications schools across the world as experts apply his precepts to the ever-changing ways we communicate with each other.

62

Robert Strange McNamara

Secretary of the Defense

Born of Irish ancestry on his father's side and Scottich-English on his mother's side on June 9, 19167 in San Francisco, Robert Strange (his mother's maiden name) McNamara was a quick learner even as a child. He could read at a thirteen year-old's level as he entered grade school. After graduating from high school in Piedmont, California with a straight "A" record, McNamara entered the University of California at Berkeley, majoring in economics and philosophy. He earned a Bacholor of Arts degree in 1937.

He went onto receive an M.B.A from Harvard University in 1939. He work for a short time after that for the accounting firm of Price Waterhouse & Company before returning to Harvard in 1940 as an assistant professor.

When the United States entered World War II McNamara volunteered for military service, but was denied active duty because nearsightedness. He remained at Harvard and taught a course for the Army Air Dorce officers while serving as special consultant to the Army Air Forces on the establishment of a statistical system to control the flow of materiel, money and personal.

McNamara travelled to England in 1943 to command a statistical control system for the Eighth Air Force. He was commissioned captain and served with the Army Air Forces in England, India, China and the Pacific and won the Legion of Merit during his active duty.

In 1946, McNamara was released from active status, having reached the rank of lieutenant colonel. He returned to the United States and went to work for Ford Motor Company. In 1949 he was promoted from manager of the company's offices of planning and financial analysis to controller. In augus of 1953 he was promoted again, this time to assistant general manager of the Ford division. He continued to move up the corporate ladder being named general manager in 1955 and vice president in charge of all car and truck divisions in 1957. Later that year he became a Ford Director and in 1960 he was elected president of Ford, succeeding Henry Ford 2d.

After serving only a couple months as president, McNamara was offered the post of secretary of defense for the President Kennedy's newly elected administration. McNamara took office on January 21, 1961.

63

George Meany

Labor Leader

George Meany started his adult life as a journeyman plumber in New York City. Long before his death in 1980, however, Meany was a recognized spokesman for all of organized labor and a man who had traveled widely to advance labor's causes.

The transition from plumber to labor leader did not come quickly. When Meany first joined the Manhattan-Bronx local of the plumber's union, he had other things on his mind. Meany had become sole support of his mother and six siblings after his father's death in 1916 and his brother's enlistment in the Army a year later. He juggled jobs both as a plumber and as a baseball catcher to support his family.

But in 1919, Meany's life began to change. He married Eugenia McMahon, who appears to have encouraged him to become active in the union. That same year, he won a seat on the local's executive board. Three years later, he moved to the post of business agent and became a full-time union official.

By 1927, Meany came to the attention of union leadership when he successfully won an injunction to defeat a lockout. He became secretary of the New York Building Trades Council, a position which brought the young union official even more notice.

The next step came in 1932, when he was chosen as one of 13 vice presidents of the New York State Federation of Labor. Two years later, he became its president. He was credited with major contributions to the effort to pass workers' compensation, unemployment and health and safety laws. His stand as a moderate also appealed to those who rejected the radical stand of some union officials.

That moderate stand and Meany's New York record attracted the attention of the American Federation of Labor, which named him secretary-treasurer in 1939. He immediately began to build public relations for the AFL through such methods as having it sponsor news broadcasts.

During World War II, Meany served as a labor representative on the National War Labor Board. He also became increasingly hostile to Communism, leading an AFL boycott of the World Federation of Trade Unions for its decision to admit Soviet trade unions and helping to create a rival organization.

Angered by Republican support of the Taft-Hartley bill, Meany worked to establish Labor's League for Political Education, which helped restore Democratic control of Congress in 1948. He was also an early backer of civil rights, threatening to remove the AFL convention from a Houston hotel unless two black delegates were admitted.

Meany's strong record as secretary-treasurer made him the prime candidate to succeed AFL president William Green when Green died in 1952. One of his first actions as president was to revive a committee to discuss reunification with the Congress of Industrial Organizations. The AFL and the CIO merged in 1955.

Meany also pushed to end corruption in the union movement. Within a year of becoming president, he had persuaded the AFL to expel the International Longshoremen's Association, accused of having ties to racketeers. Later, other allegedly corrupt unions would be expelled, including the Teamsters.

By the 1960s, however, Meany himself had become a controversial figure within the labor movement. His support of the Vietnam war and reservations about the environmental movement and feminism raised questions with some labor leaders. Others were angry with his failure to try to reverse the decline in union membership. Arthritis pushed him to resign as AFL-CIO president in 1979; he died two months later of a heart attack.

Meany sometimes reminded listeners that he was a labor leader who had never walked a picket line, organized a local or led a strike. But he was also a leader able to bring together and, for many years, hold together diverse elements of his movement to let them speak with one voice.

64

James Monroe

U.S. President

I f a man may be judged, in part, by his friends, James Monroe was a success. Through his career in politics, Monroe earned the admiration of people like Thomas Jefferson, James Madison and his administration's secretary of state, John Quincy Adams. He may never be considered one of the best American presidents, but his hard work helped build an increasingly solid foundation for his young nation.

Monroe's best-known accomplishment as president may have actually been a collaboration with the talented Adams. The two created the Monroe Doctrine, a strong statement that European colonizers should not look to the Americas for future expansion.

The team also concluded an agreement that limited arms on the Great Lakes and another securing the Florida territory for the United States.

Domestically, Monroe's accomplishments were less notable. However, his skill as an administrator and as a judge of talent for other government posts allowed the new nation to move forward confidently.

Monroe began his career in public service in 1782, winning election to the Virginia legislature. Before his election, he had studied law under Thomas Jefferson. That relationship grew into a friendship that continued until Jefferson's death.

127

In 1783, Monroe became a delegate to the Congress of the Confederation. Despite that experience, he was not chosen as a delegate to the Congress which wrote the Constitution. He came out publicly against the new document, reflecting the sentiments of his state and his own caution about any centralized government.

Once the Constitution passed, however, Monroe attempted to join the new government. He lost to Madison for a seat in the House, but was appointed to the Senate in 1790. Four years later, he left that seat to become minister to France.

Monroe's political career continued with his election as governor of Virginia. Jefferson pulled his friend back to national service, naming him to several diplomatic posts. An unsuccessful run for president against Madison moved him back to state service, but Madison again called him to Washington, naming him secretary of state in 1811. He had not lost his presidential ambitions, finally achieving that honor in the election of 1816.

As a former president, Monroe continued moving into and out of public service. He served as a visitor to the University of Virginia and as a delegate and presiding officer of the state's constitutional convention. As he had throughout his life, he continued to impress those dealing with him with his sound judgment. Monroe's circle of admirers knew they could depend on him in whatever post he held.

65

Van Morrison
Rock Musician

Van Morrison has had a career-long reputation as a very private person. But the music that he makes reaches out to the world for both its inspiration and its audience.

Morrison grew up in Belfast, Northern Ireland, hearing many kinds of music. His mother was a jazz and opera singer; that passion for jazz has influenced her son's music. Blues and American country-western were also often played. Later, Morrison would add soul, rhythm and blues, gospel and traditional Irish tunes to the mix that produces his music.

Like many rock musicians, Morrison was largely self-taught. By age 12, he was comfortable on guitar, harmonica and saxophone, and had begun singing in local clubs. Three years later, he dropped out of school and began working as a musician at American military bases in Germany.

The road to his first rock success began in 1964, when he and a group of friends formed the band Them. The band gained fame as part of the British invasion, the wave of British rock acts who dominated American music charts in the mid-'60s. Hits during its three-year history included "Here Comes the Night" and a Morrison tune, "Gloria."

With the end of his band, Morrison moved to the United States and launched a solo career. His first two "official" solo albums (an earlier record came out without his knowledge), Astral Weeks and Moondance, are still considered rock classics. Both blend many musical styles to create a distinct Morrison sound.

Critic Ralph J. Mason called Morrison's solo singing obviously jazz-influenced, and said he "wails ... He gets a quality of intensity in that wail which really hooks your mind, carries you along with his voice as it raises and falls in long, soaring lines." That intensity and that voice kept fans with Morrison through the ups and downs of future work.

By the mid-'70s, disillusionment with the music business and personal setbacks, including a divorce, led Morrison to step away from the business temporarily. His return to the public eye later that decade marked the beginning of a concern with religious themes. Those songs have met mixed reviews, although critics welcomed his efforts to, in the words of one, ground "his spiritual questing in earthier stuff." Particularly well-received was Irish Heartbeat, an album done with the traditional Celtic group, the Chieftains.

Morrison remains ambivalent about the appeal of his music to fans and other singers. While he sometimes appears to welcome their interest, he is also well-known for dodging interviews. One song title appeared to reflect his feelings, "Why Must I Always Explain?"

Even when he chooses not to explain, the music continues to earn recognition and such honors as his induction into the Rock and Roll Hall of Fame in 1993. It has also gained him a solid fan base always willing to hear how he uses many different kinds of music to express his very personal vision.

66

Daniel Patrick Moynihan

Senator, Political Leader

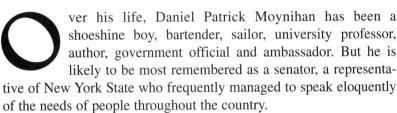

Over his life, Daniel Patrick Moynihan has been a shoeshine boy, bartender, sailor, university professor, author, government official and ambassador. But he is likely to be most remembered as a senator, a representative of New York State who frequently managed to speak eloquently of the needs of people throughout the country.

By the time Moynihan first assumed his Senate seat in 1976, he had spent almost 20 years in public life. That service started in the early 1950s, when Moynihan aided Robert F. Wagner's efforts to become New York City's mayor.

Shortly afterward, he joined the W. Averell Harriman campaign for New York governor. He left that campaign with a job on the new governor's staff. Over the next three years, he served as a special assistant, an assistant secretary and a secretary to Gov. Harriman.

While working for the governor, Moynihan met an ambitious U.S. Senator, John F. Kennedy. Impressed, he provided Kennedy's campaign with background on urban problems. Kennedy appreciated his work, and shortly after taking office, he appointed Moynihan as a special assistant to Secretary of Labor Arthur Goldberg.

Through this same period, Moynihan was also an academic. During the 1950s, he served as a lecturer at several colleges, and directed a New York State government research project.

His involvement in academics was ironic, as Moynihan had once believed he could not even afford a bachelor's degree. His later childhood was spent in poverty, after his father deserted his family in the mid-1930s. Moynihan and his siblings contributed to the family income by shining shoes and selling newspapers.

After high school, Moynihan took a job as a longshoreman. A few months later, a friend encouraged him to take the entrance exam at City College. He did so, in part, as he told an interviewer, "to prove to myself that I was as smart as I thought I was." City College agreed, and he began his studies there in 1943.

Over the next almost 20 years, a period interrupted in part by military service, Moynihan earned his bachelor's and master's degrees and his doctorate from Tufts University.

In 1963, he and sociologist Nathan Glazer published an acclaimed study on ethnicity. Two years later, he was among principal authors of a study on the problems on poor urban blacks. That study argued that the instability of black family life, the result of centuries of discrimination, was a root cause for many of the problems suffered by American blacks. That controversial work and others established Moynihan as an expert on urban and racial problems.

Moynihan continued to move in and out of government, including stints as ambassador to India and chief U.S. delegate to the United Nations. An outspoken defender of U.S. policies in the United Nation, Moynihan earned applause from the average American but suffered a loss of support from others in the administration. He resigned the U.N. post in February 1976 and announced his candidacy for the U.S. Senate in June of the same year.

Through his Senate service, he emerged as an energetic defender of families and of the Social Security program. He collided frequently with the Reagan administration, both on domestic policies and on handling of operations in Nicaragua. His positions on many of those issues has contributed to successful Senate runs in 1982, 1988 and 1994, and to his continuing legacy of public service.

67

Gerry Mulligan
Jazz artist, Composer, Band Leader

I t is an odd footnote to jazz history that Gerry Mulligan's crowning achievement, the album Birth of the Cool, is not even included in his "discography." While he was integral in arranging the scores for the historic ensemble presided over by Miles Davis, the release has the distinction of being a Davis album; his first as a leader. Recorded over a one-year span in 1949, the album would be significant in offering the world the "cool jazz" sound which would counterbalance the dominant style of the day -- bebop. Like most masterpieces, it was undervalued at the time and flopped commercially.

The performers were a young group of musical pioneers, including the 22-year-old Mulligan, the 23-year-old Davis, and musical stalwarts Max Roach, Kai Winding, J.J. Johnson, Lee Konitz and Al McKibbon. The album is a testimony to the musical dedication and sophistication of the young disciples.

Cool jazz would become especially popular on the west coast, thanks to artists like Dave Brubeck, and would redefine the genre.

Gerald Joseph Mulligan was born April 6, 1927 in Queens Village, Long Island. He showed musical promise from a young age, starting with piano and branching out into clarinet and saxophone. His song "You and Me and Love" was composed at the age of seven and he arranged "Disc Jockey Jump" for legendary drummer Gene Krupa at the age of 20.

Mulligan jumped directly from West Philadelphia Catholic High School for Boys in 1944 to his professional career, selling two arrangements to be conducted by Johnny Warrington over radio station WCAU. He was paid $35 a piece. He had a planned tour as a saxophonist fall through, but rebounded with a job arranging with Tommy Tucker's orchestra. It was during this stint he was exposed to the music of Billy Eckstine.

The young prodigy returned to Philadelphia, this time as the arranger for a new WCAU band. Through the late Charlie Parker, Mulligan performed with Dizzy Gillespie's quintet in the city.

Moving to New York City in 1946 -- at the age of 20 -- Mulligan worked with Krupa and arranger Gil Evans, who would be instrumental in helping Mulligan formulate the cool jazz sound with Birth of the Cool. Over the next few years, he would work with Davis, Parker, Stan Kenton and Benny Goodman.

Mulligan went to Los Angeles and continued to experiment with jazz sound, eliminating the piano from jazz ensembles and working as an ambassador for music. It was important for him that jazz be seen as a legitimate, respectable art form.

While critics maintain that Mulligan's early years were his most prolific and influential, he continues to record, tour, compose and arrange. He has performed with many other giants of the industry: Art Farmer, Ben Webster, Ray Brown, Stan Getz, Thelonious Monk, and, during his 1992 recording Re-Birth of the Cool, Phil Woods and Mel Torme. In truth, he must be recognized as one who has earned the right to walk among the giants.

68

Frank Murphy
U.S. Supreme Court Justice

hen President Franklin D. Roosevelt appointed his long-time friend Frank Murphy to the United States Supreme Court, he solidified the Court's liberal majority--but he also appointed a man with strong personal views that would not be swayed by politics or ideologies.

A strong, early advocate of the rights of minorities and a powerful voice against political racketeering, Murphy took the Supreme Court oath of office on Feb. 5, 1940, and immediately began making his presence known on the bench. In one of his first actions, he wrote the Supreme Court's decision striking down laws against picketing--a clear indication of the type of justice he would become.

But what makes Murphy a remarkable individual in American history, in addition to his prominence as a Supreme Court Justice, is the type of person he was and the power of his personality. An ardent Catholic, Murphy once promised his mother than he would never drink alcohol--and he never did. He also learned from his mother, the person whom he called his idol, to love all races and peoples, and he strove mightily to live up to that teaching. When his best friend, who was Jewish, was barred from a fraternity, Murphy himself refused to join it.

Roosevelt held Murphy in the highest esteem and trust, and the feeling was mutual. Murphy left a position he loved and was strongly suited to his crusader-like philosophy--that of Roosevelt's United States' Attorney General--to accept the Supreme Court appointment and help his friend, the President, advance his agenda through the nation's highest court.

To that position he brought this humble philosophy: "I should like to belong to that small company of public servants and others who are content to do some of the homely and modest of tasks of perfecting integrity in government and making government more efficient and orderly."

His political career began when he was elected Mayor of Detroit in 1930; it flourished when he was one of the earliest supporters of Roosevelt at the Chicago Democratic Convention, and a friendship was formed.

When Roosevelt was elected president, he appointed Murphy as Governor General to the Philippines in 1932; upon his return, he ran for, and became, governor of Michigan. He was defeated for re-election in 1938, in large part because he refused to enforce a court order obtained by General Motors which would have forced striking workers back to the job. That sit-down strike--at that time the largest in state history--ended after Murphy did threaten the use of troops, but his handling of the case infuriated many politicians and business leaders.

That setback opened the doors for him to be appointed by Roosevelt as Attorney General, where he became famous for his airplane raids against political racketeering across the country. He was one of the county's most active, most committed attorney generals and one of its most well-publicized.

His stint as Roosevelt's Attorney General led to his defining appointment as a member of the United States Supreme Court, where he continued his indefatigable battle against oppression, "industrial slavery" and intolerance.

69

Hugh O'Brian
Actor

Picture a western cowboy/lawman. If you grew up in the 1950s, that image might be the face of actor Hugh O'Brian. O'Brian, who actually grew up mostly in the East, started the trend toward "adult" Westerns as Wyatt Earp in ABC's "The Life and Legend of Wyatt Earp." The actor spent six seasons in the part, helping to keep the show high in viewer esteem.

The road did not lead straight to Wyatt Earp's Dodge City, however. O'Brian had started college once in Cincinnati before leaving school to enlist in the Marines during World War II. Military school training offered the experience he needed to become, at 18, one of the Corps' youngest-ever drill instructors.

The young drill instructor had hoped for overseas duty, but was encouraged instead to apply for admission to the U.S. Naval Academy. He missed the entrance requirements by a tiny margin, and was considering trying again when the war ended. With the end of the war, he ended his thoughts of a military career.

O'Brian was again considering college, this time Yale, when the acting bug finally bit him. Stories vary -- one claim is that he filled in for an ailing friend in a little theater production, decided he enjoyed the experience and launched an acting career.

No matter how he started, his greatest success came in television. O'Brian was recommended for the role of Earp because the story consultant felt he resembled the young marshal. The program premiered to good reviews in September of 1955.

Unlike some performers, O'Brian made careful choices of where to spend his television earnings. He held interests in a variety of Earp merchandise, which helped swell his bank accounts by the time the series left the air.

After Wyatt Earp, O'Brian was able to select his performances carefully. He also spent large amounts of time involved in charitable activities. That includes his Hugh O'Brian Youth Foundation, which continues to offer annual youth leadership awards.

70

Daniel O'Connell
Irish Statesman

D aniel O'Connell used the tools of British law -- the courts and the Parliament -- to shake off some of the worst ties of British rule in his native Ireland.

As a young man, O'Connell studied law in London until he was called to the Irish bar. His diary suggests he had been an able student, particularly interested in the rights of the subject under English common law.

O'Connell, one of the first Catholic lawyers permitted to practice in Ireland, quickly became known for his defense of other Catholics who were seeking emancipation from anti-Catholic laws. By the late 1820s, he was a highly successful barrister, especially known for his skill in cross-examination and in defense.

Throughout his legal career, O'Connell remained involved with organizations seeking political and social equality for Catholics. In 1823, he helped found one of those organizations, the Catholic Association, which produced a nationwide network for change.

After an attempt by the British government to ban such societies, O'Connell organized the New Catholic Association. That group gave the government further cause for alarm, scoring big victories in the general election of 1826. O'Connell himself was among those elected to Parliament.

139

His success, however, prompted additional crackdowns from the British government. For a time, he attempted to work through nondenominational groups to move forward; eventually, with changes in government, he was again able to make progress for Catholic equality.

His remaining career saw both successes and setbacks. For a short time in 1844, he was jailed for seditious conspiracy; a successful appeal freed him three months later. He also pushed the government to take measures to deal with the potato blight, but none of those efforts stopped what would become the "Great Famine." O'Connell was more successful in his arguments against the use of physical force to attain equality, and supported those who sought the emancipation of black slaves in the United States.

O'Connell's church and his nation honored him after his sudden death in 1847. A two-day funeral oration about the union of religion and liberty was delivered in his honor, at the request of Pope Pius IX. Eventually, his countrymen were to call him "the Liberator," in honor of his work for their freedom.

71

Cardinal John J. O'Connor

Cardinal, religious leader

E ven his own family said they didn't notice anything remarkable about young John O'Connor for many years -- he was a shy, "average" boy who did little to draw attention to himself. Little did they know he would grow to be a spiritual leader with a long, remarkable career.

O'Connor, born January 15, 1920, was one of five children of Thomas and Dorothy O'Connor. His grandparents had emigrated to Philadelphia, PA, from County Cork and County Roscommon in Ireland.

His teachers at West Catholic High School -- to whom he says he owes his vocation -- nicknamed him "Shadow" because he was small, shy and frail as a lad. He passed his teen years with odd jobs as a stock boy, delivery boy and finally running his own bicycle repair shop.

Classmates at St. Charles Borromeo Seminary said he "never really stood out from the crowd." It was after he was ordained a priest in 1945 that O'Connor started to branch out and pursue a diverse career. He taught at St. James High School and, while doing so, got an M.A. in advanced ethics from Villanova University. He would later get an M.A. in clinical psychology at the Catholic University of America and a Ph.D. in political science.

Coming into his own, O'Connor began work with mentally handicapped children in the early 1950s, a vocation he thought he would devote his life to at the time. However, at the outbreak of the Korean War, he requested permission to volunteer for the military chaplain corps. Chaplain O'Connor ministered to Navy and Marines corps in combat situations in both Vietnam and Korea. He did tours aboard destroyers, submarines and cruisers, becoming the first Roman Catholic priest to become senior chaplain at the U.S. Naval Academy at Annapolis. From 1975-79 he was Navy chief of chaplains.

O'Connor thrived in his leadership role in the Navy, implementing drug rehabilitation workshops, played a vital role in introducing closed-circuit television o many ships, set up moral guidance programs and wrote manuals on issues ranging from character education to leadership ethics and philosophy. He retired in 1979 as a rear admiral, complete with medals and distinctions.

Later that same year, Pope John Paul II consecrated O'Connor as bishop under Archbishop Terence Cardinal Cooke in New York. It was during this period O'Connor put his Ph.D. in political science to work writing, debating U.S. policy, and giving a voice to American bishops on international issues.

In May 1983, O'Connor became bishop of Scranton, PA, and immediately went to work opening shelters, visiting his parishioners, raising parochial teachers' wages, and making multiple television appearances.

On January 31, 1984, he became the new archbishop of New York. He took the 1.8 million Catholics under his care by storm, getting things accomplished through a blend of political savvy, a quick wit and an untiring work ethic. Above all, he commands respect and admiration from all with his impressive stature, polished speech and genuine goodwill; stepping out of the "shadows" into the glaring light of international prominence.

72

Flannery O'Connor
Writer

I n high school, Flannery O'Connor claimed her hobby was "collecting rejection slips." Long before her death at the age of 39, she had stopped collecting rejections and started collecting applause for her writing, especially for her short stories.

As her high school comment indicates, O'Connor started writing and illustrating books long before entering adulthood. At Georgia State College for Women, she considered herself a cartoonist first. However, it was her writing, submitted by a professor, that earned her a fellowship to the Writers' Workshop at the University of Iowa.

She was earning her master's degree from Iowa when her career as a published writer began in 1946. For the next six years, she found outlets for many more short stories and for her first novel, Wise Blood.

But the illness that would shorten her life made its appearance in 1950. Returning to Georgia, O'Connor was eventually diagnosed with disseminated lupus, a disease of the connective tissue. She moved to a farm near Milledgeville, Ga., living there with her mother until her death.

O'Connor continued her correspondence and travel, despite the lupus, appearing often at writers' conferences. She also completed two well-received novels, Wild Blood in 1952 and The Violent Bear it Away in 1960, plus several collections of short stories.

Throughout her life and since her death, O'Connor has been described as both a "Catholic writer" and a "southern writer." She acknowledged that both influences were important to her, but rejected either as the sole definition of her work.

Critics continue to seek that definition, many years after O'Connor's death. Perhaps it is a measure of her success that her stories continue to be read, discussed and considered, long after the author and "her" south have gone.

73

Sandra Day O'Connor
Justice

H enry Clay Day started out from his home in Vermont in the
early 1880s and headed west. He wound up settling in
Arizona, 30 years before it became a state. Little did the pioneer know that fifty years later, he would see the birth of
another pioneer -- his granddaughter, Sandra.

The woman who would become the first woman to serve on the
Supreme Court grew up on that remote Arizona settlement, learning
to round up cattle, fix tractors, ride horseback.

"I didn't do all the things boys did," she later told Time magazine.
O'Connor traveled much of her childhood, before getting her B.A.
magna cum laude from Stanford University in 1950. She earned her
LL.B. degree two years later, finishing third in her class behind
William Rehnquist.

While on the editorial board of the Stanford Law Review she met
and struck up a romance with John Jay O'Connor, whom she married
shortly after graduation.

The couple moved to Los Angeles, where O'Connor would feel a
twinge of discrimination trying to find work with a law firm. None of
the law firms had hired a woman lawyer before and O'Connor could
not break down that barrier. William French Smith, who would later
become attorney general, finally hired her as a legal secretary.

She quickly found work worthy of her talents, becoming a county deputy attorney in San Mateo, Calif. in 1952. By 1957, the O'Connor's had relocated to Arizona and in 1959, Mrs. O'Connor opened her own law firm. Meanwhile, she crammed her schedule with an enormous amount of "extracurriculars," serving on local councils and committees, assisting Arizona State Hospital, the salvation army and volunteering at local schools.

In 1965, O'Connor became assistant attorney general for Arizona. She held the post for four years before taking a seat as a replacement on the state Senate. She campaigned for the seat in 1970 and won it easily over her Democratic opponent.

As a precursor to her breaking the gender barrier on the Supreme Court, O'Connor became the first woman to be elected majority leader of her state's Senate.

The legislator made the jump to the judiciary branch when she won the judgeship of Maricopa County Superior Court in a hard-fought election in 1974. She proceeded to Arizona's Court of Appeals later in the decade.

O'Connor's rulings showed courage and restraint. She argued for decreasing the caseload of federal courts and was a staunch supporter of the Equal Rights Amendment.

Meanwhile Ronald Reagan, during his campaign for the presidency, vowed to fill one of the first Supreme Court vacancies with a woman. The newly elected president fulfilled that promise on July 7, 1980, naming Sandra Day O'Connor as an associate justice.

Eleanor Smeal, president of the National Organization for Women, hailed the nomination as a "victory for the women's movement."

Since then, she has continued to impress observers with her grace, fairness and intellectualism, distinguishing herself not as an outstanding woman judge, but as an outstanding judge.

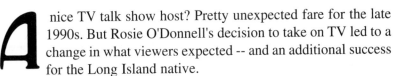

74

Rosie O'Donnell
Actress, Comedian

A nice TV talk show host? Pretty unexpected fare for the late 1990s. But Rosie O'Donnell's decision to take on TV led to a change in what viewers expected -- and an additional success for the Long Island native.

O'Donnell accepted the TV post in 1995, citing a desire to be at home more for her newly-adopted son. She was a newcomer to talk show hosting, but hardly to performing.

Her interest in the arts, O'Donnell remembered, was kindled far before her tenth birthday. Her mother, who she describes as a gifted amateur comedian, had introduced O'Donnell to the arts, including musical theatre and dance. By age 16, O'Donnell was already becoming comfortable onstage.

After her high school graduation, O'Donnell began work as a stand-up comic, covering 49 states over five years. Always, she told interviewers, she was aiming at television, movies or the theatre. Throughout that period, she ignored the misgivings of family and friends who felt she should move on to another career.

She also rejected the jealousy of some other performers.

"Some women comics when I started were jealous of other women," she told an interviewer. "They thought 'if she gets the Tonight Show, I can't.' My philosophy always was 'if she did, we can too.' ... Success breeds success."

In 1984, O'Donnell moved to Los Angeles, courtesy of winnings from the television show Star Search. There, Brandon Tartikoff, then heading NBC's entertainment division, saw her nightclub act and offered her a television role. She spent a year in the cast of NBC's Gimme a Break before it left the air in 1986.

From there, O'Donnell became a veejay on the music video channel VH-1. Later, she introduced the network's Stand-Up Spotlights, a comedy showcase, serving as executive producer and, until 1992, as host.

Her dream of movie work became reality in 1992, when she joined the cast of A League of Their Own, which told the story of the All-American Girls Professional Baseball League. Critics were divided on the movie, but nearly unanimous on the high quality of O'Donnell's performance. The same was true of her role in Sleepless in Seattle and, later, in the movie version of The Flintstones.

By 1994, she had also gotten to Broadway, playing Rizzo in a revival of the play Grease! She followed that with additional movie roles and the talk show.

For the future, O'Donnell has written several screenplays. She has made clear her interest in directing, telling one interviewer "(t)o be a director I think is the most creative an all-encompassing part of the film industry. When you're an actor, you're the paint, and when you're the director, you're the painter. I'd much rather be the painter."

No matter what she does in the entertainment business, O'Donnell says she is determined to retain a down-to-earth attitude. That determination led to a move back to New York, where, she says, living with fame is easier.

"I find that living in L.A., your whole life is centered around show business, and the more successful you become in it, the harder it is to get away from it," she told an interviewer. "In New York, they could care less. People see me and go 'Hey Rosie, how ya doing?' I go 'Hi!' and it's over."

Her career, on the other hand, may not be over for many years to come.

75

John O'Hara
Novelist, Short Story Writer

John O'Hara earned few writing awards in his life, and his relationship with critics was somewhat rocky. But the Pennsylvania native did carve out a place on the bestseller lists with what one critic described as his "irresistibly readable" work.

O'Hara was born and raised in Pottsville, in southeastern Pennsylvania. Two factors in O'Hara's childhood would show up again and again in his work: Pottsville's elite was Protestant; O'Hara's family was Irish Catholic.

"In one sense," a later critic wrote, "O'Hara's novels may thus be seen as the means by which he worked out his own ethnic resentment against the high and mighty in southeastern Pennsylvania."

That theme was immediately obvious in O'Hara's first novel, Appointment in Samarra. The novel described the tensions between Irish Catholics and elite Protestants in a fictional Pennsylvania town. Its immediate success, critical and popular, launched O'Hara's writing career. Critics call it one of O'Hara's best, showing a strength of plotting and a conciseness that was lacking in some later works.

That first novel led to a call from Hollywood, and O'Hara became a screenwriter. Again, critics varied in their assessment of O'Hara's abilities. However, his Hollywood experiences did provide O'Hara with material for two later (and best-selling) novels.

More successful was O'Hara's first effort for the Broadway stage. Working with Richard Rodgers and Lorenz Hart, he adapted his book Pal Joey to the stage; the play was an immediate hit. That success did not guarantee a bright future as a playwright, however. Future plays were not as highly regarded as Pal Joey.

About the same time, O'Hara found a major outlet for his shorter fiction. He began writing short stories for the New Yorker and was successful there until his anger over a review of one of his books caused him to break off the relationship. It would be 11 years before he again wrote for the magazine.

Through the 1950s and 1960s, O'Hara moved to longer novels, in an effort to, as he described it, "devote my energy and time to the last, simple, but big task of putting it (the early 20th-century American experience) all down as well as I knew how." Critics never agreed on how well he was able to do that. Many felt his novels sacrificed plot for detail, and they were more impressed with his short stories.

Some critics did find merit with O'Hara's efforts to chronicle America in the 20th century. One noted that "even those who disliked O'Hara's work conceded that he was a sharp social historian." O'Hara, however, disliked and rejected that label.

After O'Hara's death, critics continued to disagree on his importance as an American writer. An obituary called him "an author who never quite fulfilled the promise of his talent."

But another critic's assessment offers more promise for O'Hara's legacy. Christopher Lehmann-Haupt noted O'Hara was an author who was able to "stake out (his) own territories and draw them so accurately as to give them lives of their own." That talent, he said, may ensure that O'Hara will be long-remembered.

76

Eugene O'Neill
Noted Playwright

H is was a burning desire to write, and to write in a way no one else had written before. He despised the conventional plays and dramas of his time, preferring to utilize characters and settings that other playwrights had long ignored. He peppered his works with memorable characters and more memorable storylines, never settling for the mundane, always reaching for the unconventional.

He was, in a word, a genius, and quite possibly the greatest American playwright and dramatist in history.

Eugene O'Neill was born on October 16, 1888, in a hotel situated-ironically-on Broadway and 43rd Street. His fate appears to have been destined by genetics: his father, James, was one of America's most popular actors for almost 40 years, with a career that spanned from the 1880s until World War I.

His was an unusual childhood, with his first seven years of life spent on the road with his father, who was touring in a play, "Monte Cristo." He then went to a Catholic boarding school for six years, and subsequently spent three years in the Connecticut-based Betts Academy, before a brief stint at Princeton, where he was suspended at the end of his freshman year.

The years following his expulsion from the Ivy League school gave no indication of the greatness that was to follow. He gold-prospected in the Honduras, where he contracted a tropical fever and was sent home. He then worked in a variety of seemingly pointless jobs, dabbling in acting and reporting. But it was his job as a mule tender on a cattle steamer where he became exposed to the types of characters that would later breathe life into his work-the salty, down-to-earth characters that Americans would come to love.

In 1916, following a brief time in a sanatorium for tubercular patients, O'Neill moved to Provincetown, Massachusetts, where he came in contact with a fledgling theatre group, the Provincetown Players. This group of aspiring actors and actresses agree to produce his one-act play, "Bound East for Cardiff," and a long-time relationship was forged.

His breakthrough on Broadway occurred with the play "Beyond the Horizon" in 1920, and his career skyrocketed. That career peaked when he received the Nobel Prize in 1936-a first for an American playwright-but then began to lose its luster.

Though he continued to be pushed by his passion to write, O'Neill saw fewer of his works produced, and he toiled in relative obscurity-and in darkness-until he died in 1953. Still, his genius was evident during those dark years, as he produced such classics as "A Touch of the Poet," "More Stately Mansions, "The Iceman Cometh" and "A Long Day's Journey into Night." The majority of those works received no notice until after his death.

But his talents were recognized once again after his death, with the revival of "The Iceman Cometh" and the Broadway success of "A Long Day's Journey into Night." O'Neill had reclaimed his rightful place as one of America's greatest playwrights and drama-tists-a place he still holds today.

77

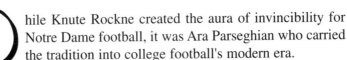

Ara Parseghian
Football Coach

hile Knute Rockne created the aura of invincibility for Notre Dame football, it was Ara Parseghian who carried the tradition into college football's modern era.

A native of Akron, Ohio, Parseghian broke the mold. When he left his head coaching job at northwestern university to take over for the Fighting Irish in 1963, it was the first time in nearly fifty years that the school hired an outsider to head the football program. He came to Notre Dame with solid credentials. His Northwestern record was 74-41-2, including four straight wins over the Irish and an upset win over Ohio State. It was with the Irish though, that he made his mark as one of college football's greatest coaches.

As is typical, raw statistics do not begin to tell of Parseghian's impact and influence at Notre Dame and in college football.

He mandated his players to live under a strict code of conduct. Notre Dame football players were never allowed to drink or smoke, not even in the off season. Enforcement was by an honor system, and the first player who dared break the code was immediately removed from the squad, permanently. It was a harsh code from a man who, as a boy in Akron, participated in and started a number of fights himself.

Parseghian also stressed conditioning and responsibility. "Football games are won by teams that are both physically and mentally alert; we will be at our peak for every game we play," he often told his players. players were also given responsibility in the Parseghian system. he was not afraid to start inexperienced men in new positions, trusting them to listen to the coaching staff and play at a high level, sacrificing their comfort level at a position for the good of the team. This combination of on-and-off the field discipline stressed by Parseghian has been as much of a trademark of the Notre Dame program as winning and is a reason why the Irish have been the benchmark for all college football programs.

Confidence and camaraderie are as essential to a top college football team as a good quarterback, and Parseghian brought both to Notre Dame. Players pulled for each other, knowing that team success was more important that individual notoriety. Parseghian wasn't beyond joining practice drills, to show players what he wanted. He made the players believe in themselves, and they in turn believed in him.

As well as creating excitement among his players and coaching staff, Parseghian had Notre Dame students buzzing about football all year round. Parseghian promised students a team that "will win football games." The excitement ran through the student body like electricity through a cable. Parseghian made sure there was constant communication between the team and the students, which built spirit to a fever pitch in South Bend.

While Rockne, Horning and others put Notre Dame football on the map, it was Ara Parseghian that made sure that the Fighting Irish would be on the tips of every college football fan's tongue every season.

78

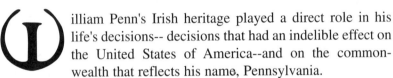

William Penn

Colonial Hero; Founder of Pennsylvania

illiam Penn's Irish heritage played a direct role in his life's decisions-- decisions that had an indelible effect on the United States of America--and on the commonwealth that reflects his name, Pennsylvania.

Penn's early life gave no prescience as to the glory and fame he would later earn: as a young man, Penn was expelled from Christ Church College in England and even spent time in prison for his flexing his yearning for religious freedom. But those formative years burned in Penn a belief in religious freedom and gave him time to hone the acclaimed writing skills that would be of such crucial importance upon his arrival in the colonies. His early writings were bold enough--and controversial enough--to earn him a stint in the feared Tower of London.

But as Penn's fervor for the Quaker religion grew, so did his yearning for greater religious freedom--a yearning he pursued in court cases in England. His first arrival in America came in 1677, when he became a trustee for West Jersey, which had come under the control of Friends (his religious group). At that time, he wrote the famous Concessions and Agreements document for the 200+ settlers who traveled with him on the ship to New Jersey.

This document provided several firsts for the colonists, all borne from Penn's difficult lessons learned in England. Among them: the right to trial by jury; protection against arbitrary imprisonment for debt; the right of petition; and the elimination of the death penalty, even for treason. Most importantly--and most pre-eminent in Penn's mind--was the refuge from religious persecution, guaranteeing that "no men, nor number of men upon earth, hath power or authority to rule over men's consciences in religious matters."

Penn also made sure there were provisions for friendly purchase of Indian lands, and even provided for equal Indian representation on juries considering matters which included Indians. Even prior to his arrival in the colonies, Penn sent the Indians a message which his reflected his Quaker roots for peace: "I have great love and regard towards you, and I desire to win and gain your love and friendship by a kind, just and peaceable life." His loyalty to the Indians was well-received and well-returned.

His impact on Pennsylvania, too, is enormous. He oversaw the laying out of Philadelphia and was instrumental in laying out the commonwealth's government. As governor of Pennsylvania, he did what he could to mitigate the evils of slavery, to assure religious tolerance and freedom, and to maintain positive relationships with the Indians.

But his major legacy is the seeds of democracy he planted in the Commonwealth of Pennsylvania--seeds that have sprouted and today continue to flourish in all of the United States.

79

Regis Philbin
Television personality

One of the most unhappy periods of Regis Philbin's life was during his stint on The Joey Bishop Show, as one main ingredient of the show was Bishop's constant belittling of Philbin. Two decades later, Philbin was poking fun at himself and gaining national recognition.

Philbin had joined the ABC variety show some thirteen years removed from college. It was his first nationwide exposure, going head-to-head with The Tonight Show starring Johnny Carson as the butt of Bishop's ridicule. One night, having been clued in to the network's plans to terminate him, Philbin walked out of a live show. Three days later, amidst a pile of supportive fan mail, the feisty Irishman returned to the show.

It was while working with Bishop that Philbin cut the song album It's Time for Regis!, which, indeed, it was. He left the show in 1969 and hosted a number of talk shows for KHJ-TV in Los Angeles. He followed that with a tour of duty in St. Louis before cohosting A.M. Los Angeles from 1975-1981.

It was while hosting the A.M. show Regis defined his own style, which to many was somewhat cruel and inappropriate. Due to his somewhat abrasive, grumpy antics, he had two separate cohosts during his stay at the program.

157

Philbin was off to New York to cohost The Morning Show at ABC-TV. Within three weeks, the show's Nielsen ratings rose from 1.0 to 3.0; the host's peculiar, obnoxious charm was beginning to catch on. When Philbin was joined by the offbeat style of new cohost Kathie Lee Gifford in 1985, the ratings climbed at a steeper pace, rivaling Donahue for ratings in the New York area. In the meantime, Philbin was given his own show, Regis Philbin's Lifestyles, on the Lifetime cable network. The show, later renamed The Regis Philbin Show, put him back in he national spotlight and led to the show that let him really let his hair down, Live with Regis and Kathie Lee.

Besides being a vehicle for Philbin's exaggerated sense of his athletic prowess, his faux-indignation, and his tongue-in-cheek self-depreciation; the show proved to be somewhat revolutionary. Each show begins with 17 minutes of "host chat" between Philbin and Gifford. It is unrehearsed, unscripted and never mutually discussed by the two previous to taping. The chemistry is genuine and utterly spontaneous -- a very courageous venture.

Gifford once told reporters: "Critics are constantly saying everybody copies everybody else; where are the fresh ideas, where is something new, something different? We think we do something completely different and very dangerous and something a lot of people don't have to courage to try every day, which is totally live, unscripted television."

Though Gifford has since left the program, the magic continues as Regis is still one of the hottest acts on TV. His success was heightened by the fabulous popularity of "Who Wants to be a Millionaire?" which played deeply on his wit and personal popularity.

Philbin, born Aug. 25, 1933 in Manhattan, has ventured out into cookbooks, videos and movie appearances, but is still defined by his unique television career.

80

Edgar Allan Poe
Poet, Writer

dgar Allan Poe's "The Raven," still one of his best-known poems, brought him fame during his lifetime. But that fame did not bring him much joy -- he spent almost his entire life struggling against loneliness, poverty and addictions.

The loneliness began very early. Within his first year, his mother, Elizabeth, had become sole parent to three children. Her own health deteriorated quickly, and she died a year later, in 1811. Her children were sent to three separate foster homes.

Edgar went to the home of merchant John Allan. For a time, he was happy there, getting affection especially from John's wife, Frances. By age 15, Edgar's literary interests and talent were beginning to shine. However, he had discovered that Allan had not been faithful to Frances, and tensions began to grow.

After high school, Edgar enrolled at the University of Virginia. His foster father's refusal to provide funds for his attendance and Poe's poor choices in handling that caused him to leave the university after one semester. Back in Allan's home, Poe made his desire for a literary career clear; after the resulting quarrel, he moved out.

Over the next few years, Poe struggled to earn a living while continuing to write and seek an audience for his work. A brief time in the Army led to an equally brief attendance at West Point.

In 1833, however, his writing attracted notice. The Baltimore Saturday Visitor presented him a $50 prize for a short story and would have given him their poetry prize as well, had they been willing to give both to one writer. The prize built Poe's reputation as a writer and led to the friendship of John P. Kennedy, who became Poe's patron. Kennedy introduced Poe to the editor of the Southern Literary Messenger, which eventually offered a staff job.

Poe proved a superb editor, but his drinking temporarily ended the Messenger position. A promise to quit drinking bought him a second chance, and he remained with the Messenger until he left for New York in 1837. He took with him his cousin Virginia, who had become his wife.

The family eventually moved to Philadelphia, where Poe took a position as editor of Burton's Gentleman's Magazine. His stories, including "The Fall of the House of Usher," appeared in Burton's. A flirtation with establishing his own magazine stalled when Graham's magazine named him editor. Again, Poe handled those duties well and watched his literary fame grow. However, his drinking, poor health and desire to start his own magazine led him to leave Graham's.

During his time in Philadelphia, Poe began refining what would later be recognized as early examples of the mystery story. Critics felt he gave those stories a method and form that established them as a separate form of fiction.

After a time, he and Virginia left for New York. There, "The Raven" was completed, drawing much favorable attention. By 1845, he became editor and, eventually, owner of the Broadway Journal. The same year, two books, Tales and The Raven and Other Poems, were published. Early the following year, however, debt, his continued drinking and both his and Virginia's bad health prompted him to close the magazine. By 1847, both nearly died of starvation; Virginia finally lost her long battle with tuberculosis.

Through the remainder of his life, bad health, drink and poverty stalked Poe. His talent continued to shine through, however, with work like "Annabel Lee." He died in Baltimore in 1849, but the work he produced through his short life lives and thrives long after his death.

81

James K. Polk
United States President

I magine a president who tells the people what he plans to do, then accomplishes just that. Unlikely? Not for James K. Polk, who managed that result in just one four-year term.

Polk, a Democrat, laid out four goals in his inaugural address in 1845. Two were related to national finances: the reduction of the tariff and the establishment of an independent treasury. The others looked to the borders of the new nation. Polk was determined to settle a boundary question over the Oregon territory and to acquire the California territory.

Perhaps the most difficult of the four goals was obtaining California. Polk had apparently intended to purchase the territory from Mexico, but that nation would not discuss the matter. Tensions escalated, leading to war in 1846. By the time the war had ended, in 1848, the United States owned California.

That triumph carried a high delayed cost. Arguments began over whether slavery would be permitted in the new territory. Polk favored a compromise, but the final answer came only with the Civil War.

Settlement was easier to reach on the Oregon boundary question. The United States and Great Britain had agreed in 1818 to share use of the land between California and Alaska. Polk, however, had run for president on a platform calling for American ownership of the entire territory. His decision to take a "bold and firm course" in the discussions eventually led the British to accept an American proposal.

Polk was not the obvious Democratic candidate in 1844. The party expected to nominate Martin Van Buren, but a political misstep left Van Buren on the wrong side of the party leader, President Andrew Jackson. Polk, long a Jackson friend and supporter, became the nominee.

The friendship with Jackson developed in Tennessee, where Polk practiced law for a short time after his graduation from the University of North Carolina. He won election to the state legislature and then to Congress, where he led forces supporting the Jackson administration. During a term as Speaker of the House, he was frequently accused of being the president's slave.

But even those who disagreed with Polk's stands frequently recognized his skills. During one bitter debate, George McDuffie gave Polk credit for debating with a "tact and skill and zeal worthy of a better cause."

That skill led his party to draft him into a run for governor, a nomination Polk accepted reluctantly. He served one term, then was defeated twice before being pulled into the presidential campaign. The work required by that office ruined his health, and he died shortly after leaving the presidency.

Polk's accomplishments have often been overlooked. But his policies brought free access to the Pacific and more than 5,000 square miles of new territory -- important additions for a growing young nation.

82

Terrence V. Powderly
Labor Leader

He rose up through the ranks to become the head of the nation's most powerful and influential labor organization, championing workers' causes decades before their time. Terrence Powderly was a true labor visionary, a man who saw the future of the labor movement and took steps he felt necessary to protect members of his organization.

In the 1880s, Powderly campaigned vigorously for the end of child labor and sought the public ownership of public utilities. He believed his organization--the Knights of Labor--was an important educational organization which should seek to effect change by educating working people to demand changes in how corporate America treated its laborers.

If Powderly had a weakness as a union leader, it was that he was more of a futurist than a pragmatist. While other leaders fought ardently for such immediate concerns as higher wages and shorter working hours, Powderly overlooked those issues, tending to focus on grander items. His most far-reaching vision was the total abolition of the wage scale; he wanted it replaced with a system in which every worker was his or her own employer. He also viewed strikes as outmoded methods of negotiation which should be replaced by arbitration.

163

His parents emigrated from County Meath, Ireland, in 1827 and eventually settled in Carbondale, Pa., where he was born. At the age of 13, he got a job as a switch-tender for the local railroad, working up eventually to car-repairer and brakeman. He apprenticed as a machinist and worked in that field until 1877, when he was chosen corresponding secretary of district assembly of the Knights of Labor, rapidly becoming the country's most powerful labor force.

A skilled orator with a booming voice, he entered politics in 1878 and won election as mayor of Scranton. He twice won re-election, serving six years in all, before he focused all of his energies on his Knights of labor career.

In 1884, he was almost appointed as the U.S. commissioner of labor, but a strong opposition to his candidacy arose and he was denied the position. He finally won a position in the McKinley administration, when he was appointed as the U.S. commissioner-general of immigration. He was removed from that office by President Roosevelt, but later was named chief of the Division of Information of the Bureau of Immigration.

A lifelong learner, Powderly studied law and, in 1894, was admitted to the bar in Pennsylvania. By 1901, he was admitted to practice before the United States Supreme Court.

Today, many of his visions are reality, including his belief that all workers must be empowered by their employers. Though his hope that all workers be their own employers has not materialized, more and more companies seek to give workers a greater say in their management--and greater control of their own destinies.

83

Tyrone Power

Actor

T he dashing actor Tyrone Power, bred of a long line of actors, needed only 18 years to score major success on the silver screen. Born May 5, 1904 in Cincinnati, Tyrone Power III was still a teenager when he signed a seven-year contract to star in pictures for Twentieth-Century Fox.

Power's grandfather was a prominent Irish comedian at London's Drury Lane in the early part of the century. Power II was a leading man in his own right on the stage.

When he was still a toddler, Power was already bouncing between New York and Hollywood to follow his parents' stage and screen jobs. He stayed in the warm climate of California between the ages of 3 and 9 due to his poor health.

His adolescent years were spent back in Ohio, where the boy worked with his father to hone his acting skills. Power's father persuaded him to join a Chicago-based Shakespeare repertory company at age 17. Later that same year, the senior Power died and Tyrone bounced between California and New York again.

Friends of the Power family helped the aspiring actor to land a role as Benvolio in Romeo and Juliet in 1935, where he was discovered. Power, eager to prove himself to his new employers, made four movies for Twentieth Century-Fox in his first year.

Power scored his first screen success in Lloyds of London [1936]. Other noteworthy films from this period are Cafe Metropole [1937], Alexander's Ragtime Band [1938] and Rose of Washington Square [1941].

With the dawn of World War II, the 28-year-old found himself in the U.S. Marine Corps. After three years of training, Lieutenant Power served in the Pacific forces. He became one of the first pilots to fly supplies to Iwo Jima when it was under nearly constant artillery fire.

Upon returning to the states in November 1945, Power struck up a new deal with Twentieth Century-Fox. He made a number of films including The Razor's Edge, The Black Rose and Rawhide. Power returned to the stage after a nine-year absence in 1950. He played the title role in a London production of the Broadway play Mister Roberts. London critic Harold Hobson called the performance "beautifully quiet and well-judged."

The handsome Power continued to star in a number of leading roles in films, following in the footsteps of his father and grandfather.

84

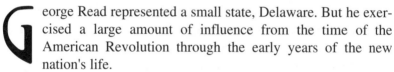

George Read

Signer of the Declaration of Independence, Delaware Official

G eorge Read represented a small state, Delaware. But he exercised a large amount of influence from the time of the American Revolution through the early years of the new nation's life.

Read was a strong supporter of the Declaration of Independence, but only after it was passed by the Second Continental Congress. Before that, he favored colonial rights but tried to avoid what he saw as extreme measures. He voted against the resolution of independence, perhaps because he saw that as an extreme measure, although records from the Congress do not explain his vote.

Even with his reservations about seeking independence, however, he was vocal in his opposition to some of Britain's actions in the colonies. He joined the protest of the Stamp Act, fought for relief for the city of Boston and helped to set up the First Continental Congress.

Before moving into public life, first as attorney general for the Lower Counties, Read practiced law for 10 years. During that time, he was married to Gertrude Ross Till, even though he believed men of ambition should never marry.

167

The marriage did not appear to dampen Read's ambition, or his willingness to serve Delaware. He was a central figure in creation of the state's new government, serving as presiding officer of the state's constitutional convention. In 1776, he was elected to the legislative council and became its speaker, meaning he was effectively Delaware's vice president.

His duties became those of acting state president in 1777, when the British captured Wilmington, Delaware, and imprisoned the state's president. Read himself barely escaped capture in crossing the Delaware. Once his family was safe, he returned to take charge of the state's war effort, raising troops, clothing and provisions. He held that post until 1778, when he asked to be relieved of the presidential duties.

Read remained in the assembly until 1779, when his health forced him to resign. While there, he drafted the act authorizing Delaware's representatives to sign the Articles of Confederation, although he had some reservations about their effects on small states. He returned to the assembly in 1782.

Over time, Read became convinced the Articles of Confederation did not provide a strong enough framework for the new nation. He favored a new government, but argued strongly that any new government had to include safeguards for the rights of smaller states. He was apparently satisfied with the safeguards in the new Constitution, and led the effort to get Delaware to ratify.

Read then moved from the state to the federal capital. He served as one of his state's first senators until 1793, when he resigned to become chief justice of Delaware. He remained in that post until his death.

George Read is perhaps not the best-known of the colonial leaders. But when you hear about the Constitution's protection for smaller states, or are reminded that Delaware was the first to ratify the Constitution, you are hearing about the legacy of George Read.

85

Ronald Reagan
President, Former Actor

Ask any 10 Americans about the presidency of Ronald Reagan, and you may get 10 separate answers. Some believe his efforts turned America around and sped the collapse of Communism. Others, equally passionate, criticize his economic policy, his "lack of compassion" and a detached management style that may have allowed lawbreaking by some in his administration.

Both sides, however, might agree with biographer Lou Cannon, who noted Reagan has "set the agenda and, on most issues, outlined the priorities." Discussion on those priorities continues long after Reagan left office.

Reagan's skill in politics and dealing with people became clear early. Both in high school and at Eureka College, he was president of the student body. As a college freshman, he successfully lobbied the administration to change a plan that would reduce the curriculum.

That experience, Reagan said, showed him that "an audience has a feel to it and, in the parlance of the theatre, that audience and I were together." He was on his way toward a lifetime of working with audiences, both in the theater and in politics.

After graduation, Reagan announced Chicago Cubs baseball games for an Iowa radio station. At the Cubs' training camp, a Warner Brothers agent offered his next career move, a movie contract

Through his acting career, he made 52 films, met both of his wives (Jane Wyman and Nancy Davis) and moved further into politics with several terms as president of the Screen Actors Guild. His experience with Communist influences in the Guild began his move toward conservatism; a later job with General Electric continued that process.

Reagan moved to the national stage in 1964 as a spokesman for the Goldwater presidential campaign. The notice he gained there eventually led to a successful race for governor of California.

Gov. Reagan focused on three issues which would later become familiar to all American voters: taxes and government spending, welfare reform and higher education. His record on all three was mixed, in part because he frequently faced a hostile state legislature. However, he was able to pass a major welfare reform act and some tax relief measures.

After an unsuccessful run in 1976, Reagan arrived at the 1980 campaign with only one opponent, George Bush. He had convinced most that a man of his age (69) would be able to seek or hold the office. As in his California race, he swamped the incumbent, Jimmy Carter.

The new president promised the country an "era of national renewal," including efforts to "get government back within its means and lighten our punitive tax burden." In foreign affairs, he pledged his administration would act "when action is necessary to preserve our national security" and would "maintain sufficient strength to prevail if need be."

Early in his first term, he was able to accomplish some of those aims, including the largest-ever tax cut, in 1981. Later, however, budget deficits, increases in unemployment and problems with deregulation and the shift of programs to the states and local government drew sharp criticism. Reagan had far less success convincing Congress to enact most of his social agenda, including opposition to abortion.

Supporters and critics spar over how much effect Reagan had on the crumbling of Communism. He maintained a stern policy toward the U.S.S.R. until late in his second term, then encouraged the reforms of Mikhail Gorbachev.

Sadly, Reagan will finish his life without understanding some of the accolades from his supporters. Several years after his 1988 retirement, he and wife Nancy announced he had been diagnosed with Alzheimer's disease. After that announcement, he withdrew from the public eye.

86

James Whitcomb Riley

Poet, writer

James Whitcomb Riley was a master with words, able to pour his words into a number of diverse forms--poems, newspaper articles, speeches, books and on the stage. He was also gifted as a painter and as a musician, but his love affair with words is his legacy.

Nothing in the early life of Riley could have predicted his amazing skill with the written or spoken word. Indeed, his parents agonized over young James' seeming indifference to reading, except for a stray book here or there. But what they--and perhaps Riley himself--did not realize was that he was developing an ear for hearing and soaking up how people spoke--the rhythm of their words, the dialect, the pacing, the word choices. He particularly learned the idiosnycnracies of how his fellow Inidana natives spoke, and often wrote in that rich dialect throughout his life.

He seemed to know no bounds to what type of work he would try in the younger stages of his life, bouncing from being a musician or actor for a traveling patent medicine show to writing a column for the local newspaper. But it soon became apparent to Riley and those around him that writing was not only his best talent, but it brought him the most joy.

In 1877, Riley showed his wry sense of humor when he published a poem in the Kokomo (Ind.) Dispatch which closely mimicked the style of pattern of Edgar Allan Poe; when his employers found out about the deception, he was immediately fired, only to find another job with the larger and more prestigious Indianapolis Journal.

171

87

Knute Rockne
Football coach

ill there be a Notre Dame without my old friend Knute? - Line from a poem written after the death of Knute Rockne

Everyone knows the "Win one for 'The Gipper'" speech. The speech, given by legendary Notre Dame head coach Knute Rockne, lives on as one of the immortal speeches of inspiration ever given. The story behind the speech is a polar opposite. A tale of tragedy - George Gipp had died from an incurable infection (incurable because their was no penicillin) and told his coach to invoke his spirit in a hopeless situation. The situation was a 1928 game against Army, where Rockne's team was trailing. The coach told his team:

"The day before he died George Gipp asked me to wait until the situation seemed hopeless and then ask a Notre Dame team to go out and beat Army for him. The is the day and you are the team."

Notre Dame defeated Army 12-6.

When Knute Rockne came to America from his home in Voss, Norway, he met the same types of discrimination that many Irish felt in the late 19th-early 20th century. In neighborhood football games, teams were usually divided up by nationality. Rockne and other

Scandinavians were usually caste together in the same group and referred to as "The Swedes" with no regard for their actual lineage. Rockne, a baptized Lutheran, came from a rich bloodline. His mother's family included doctors, teachers and clergy and his father was a craftsman. As a boy, he was "his mother's son" and his father referred to him as a klureneve (Norwegian for all thumbs). Rockne's love for football met disapproval from his father, who did not approve of his liking for American sport, namely because of the discrimination involved. This did not stop him, as he went out for football and track in high school.

On the reccomendation of a number of people, Rockne attended Notre Dame. Lonely and outcasted, due to his heritage, he packed his bags, left and returned to the campus a number of times. Rockne joined the Irish football squad where he would earn praise by making the Walter Camp All-America team. Academically, he pursued a medical tract and left Notre Dame for a high school teaching and coaching job.

His return to campus was first as chemistry professor and then, track coach. Then-football coach Jesse Harper managed to sell the idea of the Norwegian protestant as the next leader of the Irish Catholic football squad upon his retirement. A legend was born. In 13 seasons, Rockne racked up a 105-12-5 record, including five undefeated seasons and three national championships.

RKO Pictures offered the coach $50,000 after he retired to come out to the coast and give his "Gipper" speech for a movie. The plane carrying him crashed over a Kansas field, killing him. The news struck hard across America, where the funeral was covered on the radio, and in his home Norway, where he was to have been knighted.

While Ara Parsigian may have created the Notre Dame dynasty, it was Knute Rockne who put "Our Lady" and South Bend, Indiana on the map.

88

Franklin D. Roosevelt
U.S. President

 s president, Franklin D. Roosevelt faced two of the nation's most serious challenges -- the Great Depression and World War II. His legacy in handling both remains a subject of considerable debate. But that legacy also insures Roosevelt will not easily be forgotten.

Roosevelt entered politics with a surprise victory for the New York State Senate seat in a solidly Republican district around his family home. Collisions with Tammany bosses prompted him to remain in the Senate until opportunity beckoned from Washington. In gratitude for his election help, Woodrow Wilson offered Roosevelt the post of assistant secretary for the Navy. His belief in "preparedness" had the Navy ready for war before the United States entered combat.

An unsuccessful race for vice president in 1920 had convinced him to leave politics and enter business. However, an attack of polio in 1921 placed all those plans on hold. With encouragement from wife Eleanor and close friends, he fought back. By 1924, he was getting around on crutches and becoming active again in politics. Still, he hesitated when Al Smith tried to draft him as a candidate for governor. Smith persisted; Roosevelt finally agreed and won the race.

174 As governor, Roosevelt proposed measures he would later champion

as president: old age pensions, labor law reform and development of public resources. Collisions with a Republican majority in the state Legislature limited what he could achieve.

Still, his performance as governor led to the next step. In 1932, Roosevelt ran for president. Economic problems had voters longing for a change, and they gave Roosevelt a margin of 413 electoral votes over Hoover.

Two days after his inauguration, Roosevelt closed every bank in the country, allowing them to reopen only after a Treasury Department committee found them to be "sound." The administration sent a deluge of major bills to Congress. They were quickly met by opposition to what was seen as a federal power grab.

Early legislature successes included creation of the Federal Housing Administration, providing funds for rural revitalization and adding controls to the banking business. A series of Supreme Court decisions later overruled some of those measures. Those led to an ill-considered proposal by Roosevelt to enlarge the Court. He lost, but retirements eventually allowed him to reshape the Court.

Critics complained about Roosevelt's policies, Mrs. Roosevelt's travels and the marriages and careers of the five Roosevelt children. Still, the president continued to win major battles, including creation of the Fair Labor Standards Act (setting a minimum wage).

He also succeeded in convincing Congress to ease restrictions on American sales of arms to those fighting the Axis powers in Europe. Concerns about the battles there would prompt Americans to give Roosevelt an unprecedented third term in office in 1940.

By 1941, the United States was at war -- first with Japan and, less than one week later, with Germany and Italy. Roosevelt launched himself into war leadership with the same energy with which he had battled the depression. He convinced Congress to control prices and encouraged the labor unions to declare peace with employers during the war. By his 60th birthday, in 1942, polls reported 84 percent of the country was satisfied with his policies.

They remained satisfied in 1944, or at least unconvinced that another leader could better handle the war, and Roosevelt was returned for a fourth term. He did not live to finish that term, or to see the end of the war. But respect for the measures he had developed to win that war and the battle against the Depression would live long after his death.

175

89

Nolan Ryan
Retired baseball player

"**H**ow'd he ever lose?" asked one hitter of pitcher Nolan Ryan. "He throws nothing but strikes at us. He does it without effort -- that's what gets me."

Those comments were early in Ryan's storied career. By the time he retired from baseball in 1993, Ryan held more than 50 major league records, including most strikeouts (5,714), most seasons played (27) and most no-hit games (seven).

Although he had initially drawn no interest from the team in his native Texas, he finished his career with two Texas teams, the Houston Astros, from 1980 to 1988, and the Texas Rangers, from 1989 to 1993.

Ryan, the youngest of six children, took an early interest in baseball. His first pitching coach was one of his brothers, Robert.

"When I was eight years old," Ryan later said, "I knew I could throw the ball past batters." But he had much to learn about his craft. He told another interviewer that he didn't have a curve ball while pitching in high school "because nobody in town knew how to throw one."

Despite the lack of a curve ball, Ryan won 20 games and lost four in his senior year of a high school. That produced interest from the University of Texas, but was not enough to reach his real goal -- a tryout with the Astros.

Instead, he was drafted by the New York Mets late in the 1965 free agent draft and sent to their farm team in Marion, Virginia. There, he struck out 115 men in 78 innings, earning a quick promotion. His amazing ability to strike out batters continued to impress the Mets' organization, and by the end of the 1966 season, he was playing with the major leagues.

Through 1970, Ryan's playing time was clipped by injury and by his commitment to the Army Reserve. Still, he continued to impress when he did play. In 1968, he set a Mets record for strikeouts, at 14. Two years later, he broke his own record, registering 15 strikeouts in one game.

Between the two seasons, he began establishing a reputation for performing particularly well during postseason play. Strong performances by Ryan helped the Mets through the playoffs, into the World Series and, eventually, to win the World Series.

Ryan left the Mets in 1971 to begin a seven-year stint with the California Angels. He gradually developed a dangerous curve ball and continued to build his reputation as a strikeout leader. From California, he finally made it to Houston in 1980.

During his career, Ryan appeared on the American League All-Star team four times and the National League team twice. Working with co-authors, he wrote seven books, most completed during his baseball career. He and his wife raise cattle on a ranch they own near his hometown of Alvin, Texas.

Ryan is no longer terrorizing major league batters. But in towns around the country, pint-size baseball players are remembering his performance and dreaming of the time they can take over Ryan's place as the scourge of hitters.

90

Susan Sarandon

Actress

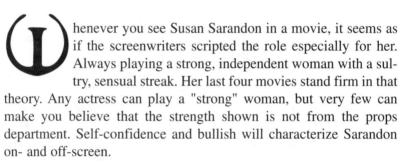

henever you see Susan Sarandon in a movie, it seems as if the screenwriters scripted the role especially for her. Always playing a strong, independent woman with a sultry, sensual streak. Her last four movies stand firm in that theory. Any actress can play a "strong" woman, but very few can make you believe that the strength shown is not from the props department. Self-confidence and bullish will characterize Sarandon on- and off-screen.

Susan Tomalin was born in New York City to a Welsh Catholic family. Family life was fairly unhappy for Susan, who was raised by a father who's own dad died during his childhood years, and by a mother who was born while her own mother was a student in boarding school. Nonetheless, her parent's blue collar background built a tough work ethic in Susan, who paid her way through Washington D.C.'s Catholic University while working as a secretary and cleaning apartments. She met her husband, Chris, in school and the two were married before she reached her senior year. A drama major with no intent of acting, Sarandon accompanied her husband to script readings in order to make him feel comfortable. On one such occasion, Sarandon was offered the female lead in a movie Joe, a movie about a teenager accidentally shot by her father.

Her early days on the silver screen brought her roles opposite Sophia Loren and found her playing Tricia Nixon in a movie about Richard Nixon. This led up to her role as pure, decent Janet Weiss in the timeless cult classic The Rocky Horror Picture Show (1978). A rock opera, Sarandon starred opposite Tim Curry, who played a transvestite vampire who kidnapped her and her newlywed husband and took their virginities. A string of failures followed, before she returned to the stage with Eileen Brennan in the play A Coupla White Chicks Sitting Around Talking (1980). A classic story of a sheltered housewife, played by Sarandon, working out her problems with the rambunctious Brennan. She would visit a similar scenario many years later.

To talk about Susan Sarandon, one must look at the role as the sultry Annie Savoy in Bull Durham (1988)-widely regarded as the part that put her on the map. A groupie of the local baseball team, Sarandon's character takes one of the local baseball player's under her wing each season to teach them the two most important aspects of life, baseball and sex.

In the early 1990's release Thelma & Louise, Sarandon teamed with Geena Davis as a pair of women who were running from deadbeat husbands, only to be marked fugitive's after the murder of Davis' rapist. This time, Sarandon played the rambunctious, take-charge woman to the passive Davis. In The Client (1994), Sarandon played a divorced, recovering alcoholic lawyer who takes over adds the role of surrogate mother to her client, a 12-year-old boy who witnessed the suicide of a mob lawyer. The heartfelt performance earned her an Academy Award nomination. 1995 saw the release of a critically successful, yet financially disastrous Safe Passage, where she is the matriarch of a largely male family whose son is presumed dead in a terrorist attack on a military base. The movie showed a range of emotion and acting talent that Sarandon possesses.

91

Mack Sennett

Comedian

F or Mack Sennett the world was truly his stage. This Irish Canadian, born Michael Sinnott, had his finger on the comedic pulse of the nation during the roaring twenties.

Sennett started out as a stage comedian with the Biograph Company. An early acting protégé of D.W. Griffith, Sennett embarked on directing comedies at Biograph from 1911 to 1912. Later having been financed by Adam Kessel and Charles O. Baumann's New York Motion Picture Company, he broke from Biograph and set up his one troupe, Keystone.

From Biograph he took with him his favorite comedian, Mabel Normand, actor Fred Mace, and actor-director Henry 'pathe' Lehrman. He also added a stock of new artists which he discovered in burlesque shows, circuses and even mental hospitals.

Keystone became know for its visual comedy. The company became popular and even enriched American folklore, all the while succeeding Sennett's only goal- to make money at comedy. Drawing on comic strips, French slapstick cinema, vaudeville and pantomime for inspiration, Keystone produced a comedy that was very different from any other theater or film of its time. Sennett's comic world remains a monument of twentieth-century popular art today.

By 1915 Sennett's company and talents ranked as one of the "big three" with his mentor, Griffith, and Thomas Ince. Griffith and Ince merged to the triangle company and later merged with Sennett to become the Triangle-Keystone company. The partnership enabled each partner to enlarge its ambitions without sacrificing any of its allegiance to slapstick or public appeal.

In the early months of the partnership Sennett went after the well known starts of the time, like his partners were doing, but soon returned to his trusted, experienced stable of actors and directors. Sennett dissolved his contract with Griffith and Ince in 1917 and the unit folded in 1919.

He lost the Keystone name in the contract disputes but retained the studio in Edendale and continued to produce films under the name of "Sennett Comedies." At this time Sennett introduced his marketing genius, the Sennett Bathing Beauties. Ornamental in films these "beauties" were used to secure publicity in magazines. Sennett found that editors were unenthusiastic to publish pictures of cross-eyed comics, however readily agreed to print pictures of young, pretty women in stylish bathing costumes. These beauties proved to be the first incarnation of the spokes models of today.

Sennett's films changed in this period as well. Ben Turpin's style of grotesque entertainment inspired him to film parodies popular films of the time. In 1921 Sennett established Mack Sennett Inc., which released films through First National. He reorganized his company many times from 1923 to 1929, when he finally decided to distribute his films through Pathe Exchange.

As time went on, Sennett's audience changed and his response was uncertain. He didn't know how to show the new public that they were not too sophisticated for the classic slap-stick that was Sennett's comic world. Initially he experimented with sound in 1928 and color in 1930.

1930 dealt Sennett another blow when Mabel Normand's life was cut short by drugs and alcohol. Normand and Sennett had a long stormy romantic history. Mack Sennett Inc. was forced to close its studio doors in 1933 do to financial problems. In 1935 the financial repercussions cost Sennett's considerable personal wealth and he was forced to retreat to Canada. He continued to produce for Fox. Sennett's curtain closed on him in 1960 as he was still mourning for his beloved Mabel, thirty years after her death.

92

William Shea
Lawyer

His vocation may have been as a lawyer, but to millions of baseball fans in New York City and across the country, William Shea will always be remembered for bringing National League baseball back to New York City.

In 1957, after the beloved Brooklyn Dodgers and New York Giants shocked the Big Apple by pulling up stakes and moving to Los Angeles and San Francisco, respectively, Mayor Robert F. Wagner appointed a committee to bring league baseball back to the city and asked Shea to head it. Wagner could not have made a more prudent choice.

Shea was a lifetime baseball enthusiast, a passion spurred by his father who took his young son to semi-pro games whenever he had the opportunity. Shea didn't see his first big-league game until his freshman year at George Washington High in Washington Heights, N.Y., where his Spanish teacher was an aunt of one of the New York Yankees' top pitchers, Herb Pennock. She motivated students by offering passes to the Yankees' games at the old Polo Grounds (Yankee Stadium wasn't off the drawing boards yet) and Shea was a frequent recipient of those passes.

He matriculated at New York University in 1926, where he received an athletic scholarship and played lacrosse and football. So impressive was he in football that Georgetown University offered him a four-year athletic scholarship, a chance he jumped at because he would be able to complete law school in that period. Shea also starred for the basketball team, and went on the play lacrosse for one of the best club teams in the country, the Crescent Athletic Club.

When Wagner tapped Shea to restore National League baseball to New York, he enlisted the services of a man who felt the city had been deeply wronged by the moves of the two franchises. "No team here lever lost money," he lamented. "It was simply a question of making more money. The most flagrant violation of loyalty to one's fans I've ever seen," he told Sports Illustrated.

She worked indefatigably to bring baseball back. First, he tried to lure an existing franchise to the city. When that failed, he tried to convince the National League to expand and grant New York a franchise. When Warren Giles, president of the National League told him in no uncertain terms that simply would not happen, Shea was undeterred.

Instead, he proposed the formation of a third league--the Continental League--and granted franchises to eight baseball-starved cities across the United States. The league was set to launch play in 1962, but Major League Baseball officials, eyeing the upstart league with apprehension, offered to add two teams each to the American and National Leagues if Shea would disband the Continental. Shea agreed, and New York and Houston were the new NL entries while Minnesota and Los Angeles got AL franchises.

To honor his contributions in bringing National League baseball back to New York, the city named the new stadium which was to be the New York Mets' home field after William Shea, an honor he richly deserved.

93

Fulton J. Sheen

Catholic Bishop

Years before anyone else know of the powerful potential of television and religion, Bishop Fulton J. Sheen not only recognized the reach television could provide as a national- al pulpit, he utilized it to become one of the most recog- nized and respected men in America.

At the peak of his career, Bishop Sheen was widely regarded as the most recognizable Roman Catholic figure in America, and second in recognition only to the Pope. In fact, he was often referred to as "the most persuasive speaker" for Roman Catholicism in the country, an honor that evolved through his writings, his radio addresses and his popular TV shows.

He was born in El Paso, Texas on May 8, 1895, the son of Newton Morris and Delia (Fulton) Sheen. His baptismal name was Peter, but he took John as his Confirmation name, later adding his mother's maiden name. His father was of Irish descent and made his living as a farmer. Early in his childhood, the family moved to Peoria, Illinois, where Bishop Sheen's formative years were spent. An early indica- tion of his oratorical skills came when his college's debate team, St. Viator, defeated Notre Dame for the first time ever while he was a member.

He received his BA from St. Viator College in 1917 and his MA from that college just two years later. In that same year, 1919, he was ordained ass a priest for the Diocese of Peoria.

His brilliance continued to shine in his dissertation, "God and Intelligence," which was hailed by one critic as "one of the most important contributions to philosophy in the present century." That, and his other work, earned for him in 1925 the Cardinal Mercier International Prize for Philosophy, then the first time that prestigious award had ever been given to an American.

After serving for a brief time as a curate of St. Patrick's Church in Peoria, Bishop Sheen joined the Catholic University of America as a philosophy instructor, a position he held for more than 23 years, leaving as a full professor.

Despite his brilliant work as an educator, Bishop Sheen is best known, though, for his magnificent radio and television sermons. Those broadcast sermons began in 1930, when the National Council of Catholic Men decided to sponsor the Catholic Hour, a weekly broadcast carried on the NBC radio network each Sunday evening.

So great was Bishop Sheen's broadcast popularity that he received 6,000 letters per day--about one-third of them from non-Catholics. He was especially effective in converting non-Catholics to Catholicism, including such famous individuals as Heywood Broun; Clare Booth Luce and Henry Ford II. Perhaps his most significant convert, though, was Colonel Horace A. Mann, who was accused of spreading anti-Catholic propaganda during the 1928 Presidential election against candidate Alfred E. Smith.

Bishop Sheen gave up his position as professor at Catholic University in 1950 to head the Society for the Propagation of the Faith, a worldwide organization which helps the Roman Catholic Church's missionary efforts.

Even today, long after his voice has been silenced by death, some of his sermons, such as "The Moral Universe," "The Cross and The Crisis" and "Modern Soul in Search of God" remain legendary and still widely listened to and read.

185

94

Alfred E. Smith

Former Governor of New York

In 1960, John F. Kennedy demonstrated that being Catholic did not mean bar someone from becoming president of the United States.

But religion had been a bar, 32 years earlier, for then-New York Gov. Alfred E. Smith. Smith lost his battle against Herbert Hoover, some observers believed, because of three things: prohibition, prejudice and prosperity, with special emphasis on the second.

A year before that campaign, a 1927 article in the Atlantic Monthly questioned whether a Catholic could serve as president.

Smith's reply was blunt: "I recognize no power in the institutions of my Church to interfere with the operations of the Constitution of the United States or the enforcement of the law of the land ... And I believe in the common brotherhood of man under the common fatherhood of God."

Opponents also focused on Smith's East Side New York background and his connections with New York's notorious Tammany Hall. Cross-country campaigning did not help; Smith lost the election and retired from politics.

Earlier political efforts were far more successful. Smith entered politics at age 22, as clerk in the office of the commissioner of jurors. His formal background did not suggest a political career; he had dropped out of high school after the eighth grade to take a job, joking later that he held only one degree, F.F.M. (Fulton Fish Market, where he had worked).

But Tom Foley, a major Tammany boss, noticed the younger man's skill with people and his poise in public and became his political mentor. In 1903, he assisted Smith in being nominated for, then winning, a seat in the New York State Assembly.

Through his early terms, Smith followed Foley's advice: "Don't speak until you have something to say ... Never promise anything that you are not perfectly sure you can deliver." He moved swiftly through the ranks, becoming majority leader of the Assembly by 1911 and speaker in 1913.

One major indication of Smith's interest in social legislation came in 1911, when he served as vice chairman of a commission investigating conditions in factories throughout the state. The legislation written after that investigation was considered to be the most enlightened labor code in the country.

By 1918, Smith was considered the Democrats' logical choice in the race for governor. He won a close contest and began his efforts, as he said, "to make good for the people of New York."

During that first term, Smith clashed with publisher William Randolph Hearst. In 1922, after two years out of office, he rejected a Tammany request to have Hearst run with him. That refusal was considered a high point of his political career.

Later terms brought most of Smith's major accomplishments as governor. He succeeded in liberalizing both the labor law and the Workers' Compensation Act, increased salaries for teachers and aid for rural schools and vetoed bills calling for loyalty tests for teachers and licensing for private schools. He also managed to get a housing relief bill and to pull the control of state highways out of the hands of politicians.

Following his unsuccessful run for president, Smith became head of the corporation operating the Empire State Building. Through the 1930s, he was a vocal critic of a former supporter, Franklin D. Roosevelt, even publicly supporting two of Roosevelt's Republican opponents. That anger eased in Roosevelt's third term as the nation moved toward World War II.

As he had throughout life, Smith spent his final years working for the people. He spent time raising funds for a variety of organizations, and was particularly vocal in supporting War Loan drives before his death in 1944.

95

Patrick

Christian saint

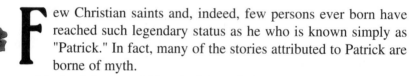

Few Christian saints and, indeed, few persons ever born have reached such legendary status as he who is known simply as "Patrick." In fact, many of the stories attributed to Patrick are borne of myth.

Much of the actual historical knowledge compiled about Patrick comes from two documents, his *Confessions* and *Letter to the Soldiers of Coroticus*. While he never drove snakes from Ireland, as stories would have us believe, the saint did perform great deeds that won him the title "apostle of the Irish."

Patrick, not himself an Irishman, was born in Great Britain around the year 390. He was raised in the country, which was still under Roman rule.

His father, Calpornious, a citizen of the Roman Empire, was a member of a district council. He was responsible for collecting taxes in his region. Patrick's father and grandfather were both Christians, but the boy's faith was unremarkable at best while growing up.

Like many saints, Patrick endured great hardship during his life; for, it was during the fourth century the invading Anglo-Saxons had pushed the Britons into Wales and the western regions of England. It was also at this time in history that Irish tribes raided the west coast of Britain to enslave its oppressed citizens. As Roman protection for the Britons decreased, the frequency of these raids increased.

At approximately the time of his 16th birthday, Patrick, his family and hundreds of others were captured and carried off to a life of slavery on the west coast of Ireland. His new, traumatic life as a herdsman was the turning point in Patrick's life. The pain put him in touch with his faith and he became aware of his loving relationship with God. To endure, the boy said hundreds of prayers each day and night.

After six years, Patrick fled his captors and returned to Britain. Approximately ten years later, he had a dream his captors were calling him back. He felt drawn to return. By this time, he had devoted himself to religious education and became a bishop in 431. He returned to Ireland at the age of 40.

While there was some Christian influence scattered throughout the country, Patrick was a pioneer in northeastern Ireland. He met resistance from the druids, but carried on his work unfurled. He made friends, preached, celebrated the mass and ordained clergy.

It was around this time the missionary wrote his *Confessions*, which gave scholars an insight into his modesty, humility and utter devotion to his faith. He characterized himself as a "fisher of men," and preached throughout the country until his death around 460.

St. Patrick's evangelical work laid the foundation for the Roman Catholic faith in Ireland and, by extension, to greater Europe.

96

Maureen Stapleton

Actress

 hen Maureen Stapleton was a girl, her "real ambition ...was to be Jean Harlow ... I always thought if I became an actress, I'd automatically look like her."

Stapleton never managed to look like Jean Harlow.

But she did become an actress, honored many times over for her skill on the stage, in movies and on television.

The Troy, N.Y., native grew up "nice, fat and unhappy," with two escapes -- "eating and going to the movies." Unlike many little girls, she pursued the desire to act to New York, arriving at age 17 with just $100 to her name. Four years later, she made her Broadway debut in Playboy of the Western World.

That launched a very successful stage career, including Tony award-winning performances in The Rose Tattoo in 1950 and the Gingerbread Lady twenty years later.

Then and later, Stapleton chose her parts with an eye toward a good script.

"The actor," she explained to an interviewer, "has to hang out his ego on the line for everyone to see and weigh. He better hang it on a good line."

Twelve years after her stage debut, Stapleton began film work with a part in Miss Lonelyhearts, for which she received an Oscar nomination. She won the award in 1982, for her performance as Emma Goldman in Reds. Other notable parts included Plaza Suite, Airport, Woody Allen's Interiors and the Cocoon films.

Stapleton rounded out her set of acting awards with a 1967 Emmy for her performance in the television production Among the Paths to Eden.

Which does she prefer? Stapleton now says her choice is film.

"It's easier," she told another interviewer. "They pay you more money. And you get two days off a week, and that's nice."

Through the years of her career, fans have been willing to give Stapleton some of that time off, as long as it means they can watch her bring another role to life.

Ed Sullivan

Television Host, Newspaper Writer

Ed Sullivan "got into television by accident," his wife explained, long after the medium had made him famous. But it's that accidental career that he will most be remembered for.

By the time Sullivan became a television host in 1947, he was already a well-known newspaper columnist. His most visible work appeared in the New York Daily News, where his column, Little Old New York, premiered in 1932. That column was syndicated to other newspapers during the 1950s.

Sullivan's interest in writing started in high school; by his middle teens, he was writing for the Port Chester Daily Item. He went to work there immediately after his high school graduation. Jumping to the New York Evening Mail in 1920, the young writer began earning by-lines and notice as a sports writer.

Sullivan moved from the Mail to the New York Evening Graphic. In 1929, after the loss of Walter Winchell, the Graphic named Sullivan its new Broadway columnist. He was not originally pleased with the assignment, but it led to a lifelong fascination with theater people.

The writer continued to increase his visibility in the city during World War II. He organized benefits to raise funds for Army Emergency Relief and the American Red Cross; CBS would later say he was the "first to organize and produce shows for wounded servicemen in New York." The United States government later honored him for that and other war work.

Sullivan had been serving for a number of years as master of ceremonies for the Harvest Moon Ball, a major dance competition. He said he did not realize the 1947 competition was televised live. A CBS executive who saw that program decided Sullivan could be their answer to Milton Berle, and hired him to host their new show "Toast of the Town." The program, which premiered in 1948, was successful from the start. It was renamed the Ed Sullivan Show in 1956.

Sullivan would later say he was "handicapped by no talent at all." However, critics noticed he did have an aptitude for locating and promoting talented artists, and he was willing to take chances on artists that others might overlook. He was among the first to present the Beatles and Elvis Presley on television.

The host was also willing to take chances with what types of artists he brought to television. In the 1950s, when entertainment was still generally segregated, he brought black entertainers to his program. Throughout the show's run, he also presented stars of ballet and opera, something very rare on American television.

In the late 1950s, Sullivan took a mix of opera stars, dancers, musicians and comics to the Soviet Union to present successful shows in two cities. Those shows were hits in Russia and later, as broadcasts, in the United States. He was credited with helping to "humanize" Russians and ease some of the fears between people of the two countries.

By the mid-1960s, however, The Ed Sullivan Show began to show its age and ratings declined. That and Sullivan's commitment to high artist fees -- driving up program costs -- led to its cancellation in 1971. He did present additional specials almost until the time of his death in 1974.

Bing Crosby once said this of Sullivan: "while he doesn't sing, dance or tell jokes, he does them equally well." But for many years, the American public welcomed this sometimes-awkward, sometimes-stone-faced man into their homes and joined him for an enjoyable evening of entertainment.

193

98

John L. Sullivan

Legendary Boxer

U ndoubtedly, John L. Sullivan loved to box, and it showed.
The indomitable boxer-known as the Boston Strongboy-plied his trade in an era when boxing was illegal in many areas, and when boxing was fought under rules that offered virtually unlimited rounds and allowed for bare-knuckle boxing.

He was a man whose courage knew no bounds, who defied all comers to fight him-and he usually won. Yet, he was a complex man, one who, at one point in his career, refused to defend his heavyweight title for approximately four years, this coming at a time when boxing titles were held until the champion was defeated, and not stripped from the champion by a boxing entity.

Sullivan became the heavyweight champion of the world in 1889, when he defeated Jake Kilrain in the 75th round of a scheduled 80-round bout. What's significant about this fight is that it was the last heavyweight title fight fought where the participants used bare knuckles; from that point on, boxers were required to wear gloves as a modest means of protection for their opponents.

But even before he eventually won the heavyweight title, Sullivan was already a boxing immortal in many respects, barnstorming the country and being arrested several times for fighting in places where it was outlawed-even being jailed for the offense.

A measure of the man's bravado, courage and swagger was his offer a $500-a princely sum when he made it in 1879-to anyone who could beat him. No one did. Further evidence of his swagger occurred for two years, beginning in 1883, when he offered attendees at circuses across the country the same $500 if they could last one round with him. No one did, and legend has it that he knocked out almost 80 men during that wily promotion.

Unfortunately for Sullivan, his reign as heavyweight champion, while elongated in years, was brief in actual title defenses. After being urged for years to defend his title, Sullivan-after perhaps drinking and eating a bit too much and not keeping in boxing shape-returned to the ring to fight Gentleman Jim Corbett in the first gloved heavyweight boxing title match in 1893. He was knocked out by Corbett in the 21st round, and lost his title.

Apparently, that was enough for Sullivan, because he never fought professionally again, instead engaging in many exhibitions for more than a decade after his only professional loss.

He died on February 2, 1918 of problems caused by his excesses. He was formally ushered into boxing immortality, however, when he was inducted into the initial class of the International Boxing Hall of Fame in 1990.

99

Oscar Wilde

Author

*S*ome of the world's greatest writers have called Ireland their birthplace. James Joyce's, author of Ulysses and other timeless works, books have gone down as literatures greatest. Regarded as one of the world's greatest dramatists, Oscar Wilde too called the "Emerald Isle" the land of his birth. As was the case with many scribes of his time, Wilde's works went mostly unnoticed until many years after his death.

Wilde, son of political activists, while known on college campuses today for his plays was once a highly-regarded poet. In 1878, he garnered accolades for his work Ravenna"while studying at Oxford University's Magdalene College. Wilde also picked up awards as a student at Portora Royal School in Ennis Killen and at Dublin's Trinity College.

Flamboyant, Wilde lived by a simple credo, he did not care what people said about him, just as long as he was being talked about. Somewhat self-centered, he was his own biggest fan. Satirists made him the butt of their cartoons and operas, but his work carried him. Admiration was widespread from British lauriats like Shaw and Harris. But his major break happened in the 1880's, when he toured America as a lecturer and producing his first play, Vera. Wilde had the heart of a modern day politician, winning new followers whenever he spoke. His U.S. tour provided a foundation for a following in the U.S.

The genius of Wilde was through his implication of his own moral system and outlandish ways of living. In Lady Windemere's Fan, the title character undertakes her daughter's misgivings and wrongdoings in order to save her reputation and that of her child's. In An Ideal Husband, he provides the idea that a woman who demands an "ideal husband" needs to be an "ideal wife" - subservient, old-fashioned and such. His most famous work, The Importance of Being Earnest, is a twisted moral tale. The story revolves around two men, each courting women who cannot and will only marry a man who's first name is Earnest. None of these plays are literary master-pieces along the lines of George Bernard Shaw or William Shakespeare, but they are the foundation of the comedic plays that would become popular in the early 20th Century.

Wilde did have a dark side to his life. Accusations of deviancy and a conviction would cloud the latter part of his life. He would find himself spending two years in prison after a libel suit he filed against a noble was overturned. The time in prison allowed Wilde to be intro-spective and sharpen his works. Many of the a fore mentioned plays were written while in prison as was the poem The Ballad of Reading Gaol, which is held in high respect as a doctrine about mans inhu-manity against his fellow man.

100

Woodrow Wilson

U.S. President

oodrow Wilson had a dream -- an international organization that could guarantee peace throughout the world. Though he saw the United States pull away from that dream before his death, the lessons learned from his effort aided Americans 30 years later in establishing the United Nations.

Wilson began to sketch principles for the organization that would become the League of Nations before World War I. Those principles were more fully developed in 1918, after the Americans had entered the war and the Germans were beginning to realize they could not win.

Through many channels, Wilson let the Germans know he would seek just treatment for them at war's end. That encouraged the Germans to surrender, and they accepted Wilson's Fourteen Points. The other Allies were initially less willing, but the Americans pointed out support here could be lost if they continued to resist. They finally accepted much of the Wilson plan.

Wilson achieved acceptance of the League of Nations during the peace conference. He could not convince the United States Senate to do the same. One major stumbling block was his initial insistence that the Senate accept the League covenant and treaty without change. Before he could reconsider, he suffered a stroke that kept him out of much of the treaty debate. That illness and his later refusal to reconsider doomed the treaty.

Wilson did not seem initially destined for politics. He briefly practiced law, then returned to the classroom -- first as a student, then as a teacher. The teaching career eventually led him back to Princeton, his alma mater.

As a college professor, he had time to write and study issues of interest. He always emphasized a careful choice of words for expressing ideas. Later, as president, he said he could "wield the sword of penetrating speech."

In 1902, Wilson became president of Princeton. He quickly introduced ideas for changing and strengthening the university. Although he was not completely successful in implementing them, his efforts drew the attention of New Jersey Democrats, who made him their candidate for governor in 1910.

Wilson continued his reform efforts as governor. Within his first year, reformers were applauding and national political leaders were wondering whether this governor might be capable of even more. He got that opportunity in 1912, defeating Theodore Roosevelt and William Howard Taft for president.

The new president's initial efforts, including an anti-trust law, were successful. By mid-1914, however, some argued that he wanted to go too fast in his reform efforts.

Those domestic efforts were slowed, in part, by foreign concerns. Before the war in Europe, Wilson worked on improving relations throughout this hemisphere and easing tensions in Mexico. Those efforts also strengthened relations with British leaders.

Through the early part of World War I, the Wilson administration struggled to keep the United States neutral. However, the German decision to sink ships around Great Britain, with no guarantee of safety for neutrals, created tension that slowly grew. For a time, Germany attempted to avoid sinking non-aligned ships. A reversal of that policy in 1917 pulled Americans into the war.

Once in, Wilson focused on victory. One commentator saw two particular strengths: his ability to create a national unity and his willingness to select good people for war-related jobs and then allow them to act. In working with the Allies, he insisted on policy independence, allowing him to advance his own ideas of a post-war world.

That post-war world would not look entirely like the one Wilson envisioned. But his ideas contributed to the path future Americans would also take toward peace.

101

William Butler Yeats

Famed Poet

He was a man of poetry and politics, a writer whose style developed and matured, but a man whose passion and private utterances were conveyed so profoundly in his work. William Butler Yeats combined two unlikely passions--politics and poetry--into one of the most remarkable literary careers on the 20th century

He was a fervent Irish nationalist, and much of his work reflected that fervor, as well as his private reflections on life and its disappointments and its mysteries.

Yeats was born in Dublin in 1865 of well-to-do parents, both of Anglo-Irish families. His father left a distinguished and lucrative legal career to become a painter, a decision that was likely the catalyst to Yeats becoming the great, insightful poet that was his fate.

He himself said that the hours spent in his father's art studio were clearly the most important in terms of his own artistic development-- the exact opposite of the impact of his education, which he deemed to be of poor quality. In fact, Yeats felt he was so ill-prepared for college that he did not matriculate at Trinity College in Dublin, instead opting to begin his career in politics and poetry.

But he was well-prepared for his careers of choice, becoming active in the efforts to begin an Irish theatre (which occurred in 1904 with the founding of the Abbey Theatre) and successfully serving in the Irish Senate from 1922-28.

Of course, Yeats is best known for his poetry, and his poetry smacks boldly of passion. Much of his early work revolved around his love for Maud Gonne, whom her pursued from 1189-1916--without success.

When she firmly refused his latest marriage proposal in 1916, Yeats married George Hyde-Lees in 1917, and have two children together: Anne and Michael.

Yeat's poems are typically laden with heavy doses of symbolism, often writing of Irish heroism and of Irish history and the country's status and future. Yeats was unafraid to lament Ireland's fate, as evidenced by this passage:

> What need you, being come to sense,
> But fumble in a greasy till
> And add the halfpence to the pence
> And prayer to shivering prayer, until
> You have dried the marrow from the bone?
> For men were born to pray and save:
> Romantic Ireland's dead and gone,
> It's with O'Leary in the grave.

Yeats' frustration with Ireland's plight in that poem from 1914 is clearly evident, but some of his other work, such as There, from his work, Supernatural Songs, is much more misty in its meaning:

> There all the barrel-hoops are knit,
> There all the serpent-tails are bit
> There all the gyres converge in one
> There all the planets drop in the Sun.

Yeats passed away in France Jan. 28, 1939, and his body was brought back to his home country in 1948 and buried under Ben Bulben in Drumcliffe Churchyard. Perhaps his epitaph, which he wrote the year before he died, best sums up his own perspective on his life--but certainly not the impact of his work on others:

> Cast a cold eye
> On life, on death
> Horseman, pass by!

pg. 15

pg. 35

pg. 25

pg. 157

Faces

pg. 147

pg. 3

pg. 178

pg. 101

pg. 169

pg. 145

Faces

pg. 129

pg. 65

pg. 176